Mass Media

Other Books of Related Interest:

Opposing Viewpoints Series

Media Violence

At Issue Series

Is Racism a Serious Problem?

Current Controversies Series

Media Ethics

"Congress shall make
no law ... abridging
the freedom of speech,
or of the press."

First Amendment to the U.S. Constitution

The basic foundation of our democracy is the First Amendment guarantee of freedom of expression. The Opposing Viewpoints Series is dedicated to the concept of this basic freedom and the idea that it is more important to practice it than to enshrine it.

OPPOSING VIEWPOINTS® SERIES

Mass Media

Roman Espejo, Book Editor

GREENHAVEN PRESS
A part of Gale, Cengage Learning

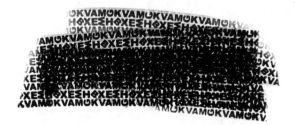

GALE
CENGAGE Learning™

Detroit • New York • San Francisco • New Haven, Conn • Waterville, Maine • London

Christine Nasso, *Publisher*
Elizabeth Des Chenes, *Managing Editor*

© 2010 Greenhaven Press, a part of Gale, Cengage Learning.

Gale and Greenhaven Press are registered trademarks used herein under license.

For more information, contact:
Greenhaven Press
27500 Drake Rd.
Farmington Hills, MI 48331-3535
Or you can visit our Internet site at gale.cengage.com

For product information and technology assistance, contact us at

Gale Customer Support, 1-800-877-4253
For permission to use material from this text or product, submit all requests online at
www.cengage.com/permissions

Further permissions questions can be emailed to permissionrequest@cengage.com

Articles in Greenhaven Press anthologies are often edited for length to meet page requirements. In addition, original titles of these works are changed to clearly present the main thesis and to explicitly indicate the author's opinion. Every effort is made to ensure that Greenhaven Press accurately reflects the original intent of the authors. Every effort has been made to trace the owners of copyrighted material.

Cover Image copyright © iStockPhoto.com/iLexx.

LIBRARY OF CONGRESS CATALOGING-IN-PUBLICATION DATA

Mass media / Roman Espejo, book editor.
    p. cm. -- (Opposing viewpoints)
    Includes bibliographical references and index.
    ISBN 978-0-7377-4530-6 (hardcover)
    ISBN 978-0-7377-4531-3 (pbk.)
    1. Public health. 2. Mass media I. Espejo, Roman.
    P87.25.M37 2009
    302.23--dc22   2009023849

Printed in the United States of America
2 3 4 5 6 7 13 12 11 10 09

Contents

Chapter 3: How Does the Media Affect Society?

Chapter 4: How Will the Media Be Affected by the Internet?

Why Consider Opposing Viewpoints?

> *"The only way in which a human being can make some approach to knowing the whole of a subject is by hearing what can be said about it by persons of every variety of opinion and studying all modes in which it can be looked at by every character of mind. No wise man ever acquired his wisdom in any mode but this."*
>
> John Stuart Mill

In our media-intensive culture it is not difficult to find differing opinions. Thousands of newspapers and magazines and dozens of radio and television talk shows resound with differing points of view. The difficulty lies in deciding which opinion to agree with and which "experts" seem the most credible. The more inundated we become with differing opinions and claims, the more essential it is to hone critical reading and thinking skills to evaluate these ideas. Opposing Viewpoints books address this problem directly by presenting stimulating debates that can be used to enhance and teach these skills. The varied opinions contained in each book examine many different aspects of a single issue. While examining these conveniently edited opposing views, readers can develop critical thinking skills such as the ability to compare and contrast authors' credibility, facts, argumentation styles, use of persuasive techniques, and other stylistic tools. In short, the Opposing Viewpoints Series is an ideal way to attain the higher-level thinking and reading skills so essential in a culture of diverse and contradictory opinions.

In addition to providing a tool for critical thinking, Opposing Viewpoints books challenge readers to question their own strongly held opinions and assumptions. Most people form their opinions on the basis of upbringing, peer pressure, and personal, cultural, or professional bias. By reading carefully balanced opposing views, readers must directly confront new ideas as well as the opinions of those with whom they disagree. This is not to simplistically argue that everyone who reads opposing views will—or should—change his or her opinion. Instead, the series enhances readers' understanding of their own views by encouraging confrontation with opposing ideas. Careful examination of others' views can lead to the readers' understanding of the logical inconsistencies in their own opinions, perspective on why they hold an opinion, and the consideration of the possibility that their opinion requires further evaluation.

Evaluating Other Opinions

To ensure that this type of examination occurs, Opposing Viewpoints books present all types of opinions. Prominent spokespeople on different sides of each issue as well as well-known professionals from many disciplines challenge the reader. An additional goal of the series is to provide a forum for other, less known, or even unpopular viewpoints. The opinion of an ordinary person who has had to make the decision to cut off life support from a terminally ill relative, for example, may be just as valuable and provide just as much insight as a medical ethicist's professional opinion. The editors have two additional purposes in including these less known views. One, the editors encourage readers to respect others' opinions—even when not enhanced by professional credibility. It is only by reading or listening to and objectively evaluating others' ideas that one can determine whether they are worthy of consideration. Two, the inclusion of such viewpoints encourages the important critical thinking skill of objectively evaluating an author's credentials and bias. This evaluation will illuminate an author's reasons for taking a particular stance on an issue and will aid in readers' evaluation of the author's ideas.

It is our hope that these books will give readers a deeper understanding of the issues debated and an appreciation of the complexity of even seemingly simple issues when good and honest people disagree. This awareness is particularly important in a democratic society such as ours in which people enter into public debate to determine the common good. Those with whom one disagrees should not be regarded as enemies but rather as people whose views deserve careful examination and may shed light on one's own.

Thomas Jefferson once said that "difference of opinion leads to inquiry, and inquiry to truth." Jefferson, a broadly educated man, argued that "if a nation expects to be ignorant and free . . . it expects what never was and never will be." As individuals and as a nation, it is imperative that we consider the opinions of others and examine them with skill and discernment. The Opposing Viewpoints Series is intended to help readers achieve this goal.

David L. Bender and Bruno Leone,
Founders

Introduction

"The recent wave of concentration is reducing global media to basically a few mega-corporations. And of course, the effects of that on freedom and democracy barely have to be discussed. They're obvious."

Noam Chomsky

"At a time when such a fragmented audience is dividing itself . . . it may even be socially positive that there are some mass audience shows, movies, and books . . . [that] give us something common to talk about."

Ben Compaine

The scope of today's mass media is mind-boggling. Numerous television series, such as *Big Brother* and *America's Next Top Model,* have been adapted and launched in dozens of nations, from Bulgaria to the Philippines. The acclaimed British film *Slumdog Millionaire* brought international fame to child actors Rubina Ali and Azharuddin Mohammed Ismail, who hail from the slums of Mumbai, India. Yahoo!, one of the most visited Web sites, offers the world's 1.6 billion Internet users customized interfaces in more than thirty countries. And the Associated Press, an American news outlet, reaches more than half the global population every day, through more than 1,700 newspapers and 5,000 radio and television stations in the United States alone.

For some critics, the pervasiveness of television, film, radio, publishing, and the World Wide Web is a harmful part of globalization. According to the *Stanford Encyclopedia of Philosophy*, the term "globalization" often is synonymous with "westernization" and "Americanization," or "the growing dominance of western (or even American) forms of political, economic, and cultural life." Indeed, some scholars identify far-reaching mass media as a catalyst for protest and violence against the West. Ehsan Ahrari, an external researcher for the Strategic Studies Institute, states in *FinalCall.com News* in May 2006 that the dissemination of allegedly anti-Islamic American news, information, and entertainment is known within the Muslim world as a "war of ideas." The phrase "became quite profound in the aftermath of the terrorist attacks of September 11, 2001, on the United States," Ahrari adds.

Therefore, some observers believe that the mass media has become a dominant force of globalization with alarming repercussions. As British writer Katherine Ainger argues in an April 2001 *New Internationalist* article, "[T]he globalizing conquistadores of the 21st century are the media giants of cultural capitalism—Disney, AOL Time Warner, Sony, Bertelsmann, News Corporation, Viacom, Vivendi Universal." She alleges that "in every country media corporations help to break our relationships to our communities, educators, collective cultures, experiences. They turn us into isolated consumers—and then sell our stories back to us." Other observers contend that these conglomerates threaten free thinking, cultural identity, and communication. In a January 2000 *Los Angeles Times* article American economist Jeremy Rifkin declares,

Transnational media companies with communications networks that span the globe are mining local cultural resources in every part of the world and repackaging them as cultural commodities and entertainments. . . . By controlling the pipelines that people use to communicate with one another, as well as shaping much of the cultural content that is filmed, broadcast on television, or sent over the Internet, companies such as AOL-Time Warner are able to affect the experiences of people everywhere. Moreover, there is no precedent in history for such overarching control of human communications.

By contrast, detractors refute claims that the mass media is singularly westernized or American. Stephen Galloway, contributing editor to *Hollywood Reporter*, proposes in a November 2003 article that the power to globalize through media is changing hands, "At this point, the key figures leading the media sector in the years ahead are as likely to come from India and South Korea as they are from Europe or America." For example, he contends that the output of India's film industry, which releases hundreds of features a year, surpasses that of the United States. In fact, Galloway asserts that "Hollywood can no more live in 'splendid isolation' than can the nation as a whole—and the industry is discovering how connected it is to the world at large."

Others state that the growing mass media contributes to communities and the sharing of cultures. Virginia Postrel, a columnist for *Atlantic*, states in a November 1994 *Reason* article, "[M]edia make more editors, and more communities, possible," continuing that "media communities don't just break up the common culture into subcultures. They allow outsiders to peek into communities of thought by visiting their media." Moreover, proponents speculate that globally distributed television programs, movies, and other content establish a worldwide common ground. Blogger Michael Jennings writes in a December 2003 post on Samizdata.net, "[T]he globalised world in which I, an Australian, who lives in London, can spontaneously start singing a song from a musical episode of a television series [*Buffy the Vampire Slayer*] of light gothic horror set in a Californian high school with a beautiful, somewhat anglicised Argentine woman in an underground train station in Antwerp is something I like immensely."

The effects of mass media on politics and society, as well as communities and individuals, remain controversial issues.

The debates will only intensify as technologies improve and broadcast ownership rules are reconsidered, bringing changes to the press, entertainment and advertising industries, and to the flow of information. *Opposing Viewpoints: Mass Media* examines these and other topics in the following chapters: Is Bias in the Media a Serious Problem? Does Media Ownership Need More or Less Regulation? How Does the Media Affect Society? How Will the Media Be Affected by the Internet? With their broad range of opinion, theories, and statistics, the authors of this volume bring the controversies of mass media to the forefront.

OPPOSING
VIEWPOINTS®
SERIES

CHAPTER 1

Is Bias in the Media a Serious Problem?

Chapter Preface

Dubbed "Missing White Woman Syndrome," numerous observers assert that the disappearances, abductions, and homicides of young female Caucasians attract a disproportionate amount of press attention. According to the National Center for Missing Adults (NCMA), "Unless, it's a pretty girl aged 20 to 35, the media exposure is just not there." This includes news coverage of the tragic and mysterious cases of former Washington intern Chandra Levy, high school student Natalee Holloway, and pregnant Lacie Peterson.

Some believe that because of underlying racism and other biases, missing nonwhite women and children are also missing from the news. For instance, Roy Peter Clark, senior scholar at the Poynter Institute for Media Studies, maintains in a July 2004 report by Alex Johnson on msnbc.com that the "victims that get the most coverage are female rather than male. They are white, in general, rather than young people of color. They are at least middle class, if not upper middle class." In fact, Clark contends that Missing White Woman Syndrome reveals a "perverted, racist view of the world" where "white is good; black is bad." And when *Essence* magazine profiled missing African American women in a 2005 article, it stated that "[w]hen black women disappear, the media silence can be deafening."

Some statistics, however, may offer evidence that frequent stories of missing or murdered white women and girls reflect a grim reality, not a media phenomenon. A U.S. Department of Justice study claims that 80 percent of abductees between twelve and seventeen years of age are white females. In addition, the Federal Bureau of Investigations (FBI) considers this category of missing persons to be most likely held against their will and in most danger of being assaulted and killed.

Missing White Woman Syndrome is one of the several types of alleged bias that are debated by media watchdogs, political pundits, and journalists. In the following chapter, the authors deliberate the objectivity and neutrality of reporters, television and radio networks, news organizations, and the news itself.

> *"Conservatives and Republicans are be-*
> *ing shortchanged in terms of their rep-*
> *resentation in the media."*

Liberal Media Bias Is a Serious Problem

Andrew G. Selepak

The increasing perception of liberal media bias reflects audiences'
growing skepticism of mainstream news organizations, writes
Andrew G. Selepak in the following viewpoint. According to
Selepak, a major poll on the media reveals that increasing num-
bers of Americans do not "trust" news outlets and believe they
are "out of touch." Additionally, the author claims his recent
study, which supports conservatives' dissatisfaction with the me-
dia (and, conversely, liberals' satisfaction), suggests that Republi-
can and conservative views suffer from unequal representation in
the news, tarnishing the media's credibility. Selepak is a writer
for Accuracy in Media, a not-for-profit citizens media watchdog
organization based in Washington, DC.

As you read, consider the following questions:

1. In the author's opinion, how have American views of
   election media coverage changed?

Andrew G. Selepak, "AIM Report: New Evidence of Liberal Media Bias—November A," *Accuracy in Media*, November 6, 2006. Copyright © 2006 Accuracy in Media. All rights reserved. Reproduced by permission.

2. Why does Selepak compare Fox and CNN?

3. How does Selepak support his assertion that liberals and Democrats dominate mass media?

(E)ditor's Note: This study found evidence that conservatives were more likely to perceive media bias than liberals, but that both conservatives and liberals detected bias in media outlets that leaned against their political perspectives. In the end, however, because conservatives were more critical of the media both in general and in response to specific outlets, the results seem most consistent with the claim that a liberal political bias exists in the mainstream news media.)

Claims of media bias are not new, but increasing claims of bias, especially a perceived liberal media bias, have led to diminishing credibility ratings among news outlets, and an increased level of skepticism of all news coverage.

A 2004 study by the Pew Research Center for the People and the Press showed that 53% of Americans agreed with the statement, "I often don't trust what news organizations are saying," and 48% believe that the people who decide on news content are "out of touch," and those numbers are rising. In 1987, 62% of the public believed election coverage was free of partisan bias, down to 53% in 1996, 48% in 2000, and 38% by 2004.

Research suggests that when equal and opposing views are presented in an objective news story, some observers may deem half the story as inaccurate and thus biased, instead of balanced. However, if objective reporting is the cause of perceived bias, there should be an equal number of claims of bias from conservatives and liberals, and both sides should be equally distrustful of the news. However, previous research shows this to not be the case, as conservatives overwhelmingly make more charges of bias in the media than their liberal counterparts.

Conservative claims of a liberal media bias are having an impact upon public perceptions of news coverage. According to research by the Pew Center, this led to an overall audience decrease for many of the major broadcast and cable television outlets and a perceived decrease in credibility for the news as a whole. Republicans have turned from traditional news sources to additional media such as Rush Limbaugh's radio program, Bill O'Reilly's TV and radio programs, and the Fox News Channel, while Democrats' viewing habits have remained mostly unchanged. This shift by the Republican audience has led to an overall polarization between where Republicans and Democrats obtain their news, with Republicans, and more specifically conservatives, becoming increasingly distrustful of the mainstream media.

Perceived Bias

Republicans, however, are not alone in perceiving media bias. Studies find that claims of a media bias favoring Republicans are increasing among Democrats as well, up to 29% in 2004 from 19% in 2000. In 2004, a majority of independents reported that there is a bias in news tilted toward one political party or another, 57% up from 49% in 2000; though independents are divided as to which party the coverage favors. Yet, despite the number of claims of bias in the media, a survey conducted by the Pew Center found that 67% of Americans report they prefer to receive unbiased news, while only 25% of Americans report being in favor of news reflecting their political leanings. To understand why the perception of bias has increased, it is important to understand how researchers define bias, and how it is being perceived in the media.

Bias is defined in one study as a "perceived attribute of a news source whereby the individual news source, or the group the news source represents, has a clear vested interest in a cause or action relative to maintaining or changing the status quo ... (and) a biased journalistic perspective, then, would mean only one side, not two or more sides, of an issue is presented."

Perception of bias is associated with the perception of accuracy and credibility, and a decrease in a news sources' credibility renders that source less useful; as perceived credibility declines, conceivably, so does the audience. Since 2002, only the Fox News Channel has seen a growth in viewership, mainly from a growing Republican audience, while other news and cable outlets have seen their audience share go flat if not decline. Most notable is CNN, whose credibility rating among Republicans dropped from 33% in 2000 to 26% in 2004, and the percentage of people watching CNN dropped from 35% of the U.S. population in 1993, to 22% in 2004.

Fox vs. CNN

By comparison, the Fox News Channel's credibility rating moved up from 26% in 2000 to 29% in 2004, and the percentage of people who watch Fox News rose from 17% in 1998 to 25% in 2004, giving the Fox News Channel a larger audience than CNN. The Fox News Channel has become Republicans' most credible source for the news among television and cable news outlets, and CNN is now Republicans' second most trusted source.

Among Democrats, CNN's credibility rating was 48% in 2000 and by 2004 that number dropped only slightly to 45%, remaining Democrats' most credible news source. Meanwhile, in 2000, the Fox News Channel received a 27% credibility rating among Democrats, with a slight drop to 24% by 2004, to become Democrats' least trusted news source among television and cable news outlets.

The above trend remains constant for print outlets as well. Democrats find the major print outlets to be more credible than Republicans, with the *New York Times* having the most noticeable disparity between Republicans and Democrats. In

2004 the Pew Center found that the *New York Times* received a credibility score from Republicans of 14% compared to Democrats with 31%. Republicans' perceived bias of the *New York Times* is most likely caused by the *Time*'s reputation for a relatively liberal editorial page, and because the paper has not endorsed a Republican Presidential candidate since [Dwight D.] Eisenhower in 1956.

Conservatives justify their belief that a liberal media bias exists by arguing that journalists are liberal, and that their ideology affects how journalists cover the news. For example, a survey in 1992 showed that 89% of Washington, DC, journalists voted for President [Bill] Clinton in the 1992 Presidential election. These results may explain why throughout 1992, the Center for Media and Public Affairs (CMPA) found that more than 70% of the networks' sound-bites about President [George H.W.] Bush were negative, whereas the majority of sound-bites about Governor Clinton were positive.

Before the 2004 election, the CMPA released a report that showed that on broadcast TV networks and weekly news magazines, evaluations of Sen. [John] Kerry were positive by a 2-to-1 margin, and that over 60% of evaluations of President [George W.] Bush were negative.

Some scholars contend that journalists seek a more activist role in reporting, and that this, combined with a liberal slant, produces a liberal media bias.

New Study

To test perceptions of media bias, this study concentrated on two important questions. First, will conservatives perceive more media bias than liberals? Second, will conservatives and liberals have opposite perceptions of bias concerning individual media outlets? To test these two issues, participants were asked to answer a survey and forward it to other members of the general public. The survey measured an individual's perception of media bias and political ideology. This led to a return of 169 usable surveys of adults, 18 and over.

Only four demographic questions were asked of participants. These questions were included to determine if gender, race, income, or education demographics might affect perceptions of bias. In addition, the question of, "In politics TODAY, do you consider yourself a Republican, Democrat, or Independent?" was also asked as a check on the Political Ideology Score. In response to the question, 39.1% of participants considered themselves Democrats, 32.5% Republicans, and 28.4% Independents, creating a rough one-third distribution.

Perceived media bias was measured using seven questions whose scores were combined to achieve an overall media bias perception score. The format was based on previous research, and scores were measured on a scale from strongly disagree to strongly agree.

Participants were asked if they believed the news was biased against their views, if their issues were presented accurately in the media, if most news stories were presented in a balanced and fair manner, if news stories usually quote at least two sources, and if they believed Network Television news, editorial pages in National Newspapers, and Talk Radio were biased against their views. The scores from each question were combined and the total created the participants' perception of bias in the media score, where a higher score represented a higher perception of bias in the media. When tested, the scores achieved a normal distribution but slightly skewed toward a greater overall perception of bias in the media.

Methodology

To determine political persuasion, each participant was asked to choose a position, from strongly agree to strongly disagree, among a list of ten issues. For each issue listed the option of "neutral or no opinion" was given. A response of No Opinion was considered ideological ambivalence about an issue.

Among the ten issues, liberals were presumed to Strongly Agree with universal health care, embryonic stem cell research, Affirmative Action in college admissions, labor unions, and being Pro-Choice. Conservatives were presumed to Strongly Agree with allowing school prayer, an amendment to ban same-sex marriages, banning inappropriate books from public libraries, using the military to ensure peace, and in favor of the death penalty.

The scores from each question were cumulated on a scale where the lower the score, the more conservative, the higher the score, the more liberal, and middle scores were equated with political moderation. Using participants' Political Ideology Scores and Perception of Bias Scores, a statistical test showed that conservatives did perceive more bias in the news media than liberals. In other words, the more conservative the respondent, the more likely he or she saw bias in the media.

Testing News Organizations

The final analysis determined if conservatives and liberals find different media outlets biased against their views. To test this theory, participants were asked which, among eight different news outlets, they believed were biased against their political and social beliefs. Responses ranged from Strongly Agree to Strongly Disagree. The outlets were *Newsweek*, the Rush Limbaugh radio program, the *Daily Show* with Jon Stewart, the Fox News Channel, CNN, *60 Minutes*, the *Washington Post*, and the *New York Times*.

To test the eight outlets, each participant's Political Ideology Score was recoded to create distinctive categories of conservative, moderate and liberal. A one-third breakdown was used to roughly match the demographic party affiliation responses. Next, a statistical table was generated for each outlet to determine how the three groups evaluated that outlet's political leanings. Finally, an analysis of each table was conducted to tell if the difference in evaluations was statistically significant.

No Fair Shake on the Economy

The press simply doesn't give the Right a fair shake on the economy. In an important econometric study, American Enterprise Institute researchers Kevin Hassett and John Lott methodically surveyed headlines in hundreds of newspapers and AP [Associated Press] reports on unemployment, GDP [gross domestic product], retail sales, and durable-goods orders going back to 1985, and found them to be considerably gloomier overall when a Republican sat in the White House, regardless of the economic data the stories reported. For the same kind of economic news, Republican presidents received about 20 to 30 percent less positive coverage from the nation's ten leading papers.

Brian C. Anderson, South Park Conservatives:
The Revolt Against Liberal Media Bias.
Washington, DC: Regnery Publishing, 2005.

Among all eight media outlets, conservatives and liberals had opposing views on which outlets were biased against their views, with all eight results being statistically significant. It is important to note that liberals found some outlets biased while conservatives did not, and with the exceptions of CNN and Fox News, a majority of moderates had no opinion.

The results from this study suggests that conservatives do in fact perceive more bias than liberals, and conservatives and liberals perceive opposing news outlets to be biased against their views. The results also show that on the whole, liberals are generally happy with the media, which may explain why conservatives are more likely to perceive a media bias.

With liberals being happy with the media, and because conservatives perceive a general media bias, the study suggests that the media in fact are liberal. This study did not prove the existence of bias in the media, but it does suggest that a bias does exist because perception is reality. Liberals and conservatives did perceive bias, and that perception of bias leads to the reality of bias, which depending on the outlet can be either liberal or conservative.

Although by sex the sample was fairly evenly split, overall the sample skewed toward being more affluent, educated, and white than was expected, and thus vastly different from the general population. Therefore, care should be taken before drawing inferences to the general population. Men and women were tested separately, but there was no statistical evidence to show that gender had any effect on perceptions of bias. As for the other demographic differences, although important, they were not examined independently.

One issue that occurred was that participants in general answered numerous pro-liberal questions with pro-liberal responses which skewed the sample to be more liberal. However, this problem may have been caused by the wording of the questions. For example, 80.5% of participants agreed or strongly agreed that abortion should remain a legal medical procedure; a more appropriate question might have been to ask about Partial Birth Abortions. The questions were chosen in the hopes of having a 1/3 breakdown, but regardless of how participants viewed the question, their answers were not interpreted and instead recorded as marked because the questions were selected from published articles using the intentions of the original researchers.

The Key Test

Although this study found that being a conservative significantly led to a higher perception of bias than in liberals or moderates, the result does not settle the issue of whether conservatives are "trained" to see bias where none exists, or if conservatives have good reason to see bias in a "liberal" media.

To test this, it was important to determine if conservatives found all of the news outlets used for this study to be biased, while liberals found no news outlets to be biased, then there would be statistical evidence that a pseudo-paranoia exists among conservatives that the news media is biased against them.

However, conservatives did not perceive every outlet as biased against them. Not surprisingly, only the Fox News Channel and Rush Limbaugh's radio program were seen by conservatives as not being biased against their views, while a majority of liberals found both to be biased. Conversely, *Newsweek*, the *Daily Show*, CNN, *60 Minutes*, the *Washington Post*, and the *New York Times* were perceived as having a bias by conservatives, while liberals did not find these outlets to be biased. Although these results are consistent with previous research, this study though added that on two outlets, CNN and Fox News, a majority of political moderates disagreed they were biased against their beliefs; this suggests that to an "impartial observer," these were the most objective outlets tested.

Although these results do not prove that any of the media outlets named hold a particular leaning or are biased in any way, the results do suggest that conservative and liberal individuals perceive certain news outlets to be biased against their views, while other outlets are either less biased or in agreement with their views. This could suggest that conservatives and liberals perceive opposing news outlets as biased against their beliefs because their views of reality do not correspond to the views presented by the media outlets.

This study offers a response to the media's own defense of, "We must be doing a good job if we're getting it from both sides." The problem is that the media are not getting it from both sides; they are getting it from one side.

Liberals, on the whole, are pretty happy with the media, especially the mainstream media. Meanwhile, this study shows that being a conservative significantly led to a greater perception of media bias, and as credibility declines, so too does the audience.

So as long as conservatives continue to perceive a liberal bias in the mainstream media, conservatives will seek out other news outlets for their news and information which will lead to an ever decreasing audience for the mainstream media that espouse beliefs contrary to the audience.

Affirmative Action for Conservatives?

A new survey confirms that liberals and Democrats dominate the major media.

The website of the Project for Excellence in Journalism (PEJ) reports the findings from a new book, *The American Journalist in the 21st Century: US News People at the Dawn of a New Millennium*. It finds that 40 percent of journalists described themselves as being on the left side of the political spectrum and conservatives were only 25 percent. Moderates made up 33 percent.

In terms of political party affiliation, 36 percent of journalists said they were Democrats, but only 18 percent said they were Republicans.

Viewed in context, citing Gallup poll data on the ideological make-up of the public, the article on the PEJ website says that 40 percent of the journalists are liberal but only 17 percent of the public is. While 41 percent of the public is conservative, only 25 percent of the journalists are. That means there is a tremendous gulf in terms of the political views of journalists and the public.

The People vs. the Press

That also means that conservatives and Republicans are being shortchanged in terms of their representation in the media. But don't look for any affirmative action program to make up the difference. Our media, you see, are interested in hiring liberal journalists representing different sexual orientations or ethnic backgrounds, but philosophical diversity is something that is off the table.

> "When it comes to the nation's op-ed pages, it is the progressives who are getting the short end of the stick."

Conservative Media Bias Is a Serious Problem

Media Matters for America

Media Matters for America (MMFA) is a Web-based, not-for-profit information and research center that monitors conservative media. Countering claims that liberal media bias is prevalent, MMFA contends in the following viewpoint that conservatives command the majority of columns in the nation's newspapers. According to MMFA's report, for every single newspaper that presents more progressive views, three run more conservative views. MMFA also maintains that conservative voices have the overall edge in newspapers, despite stark political differences and voting patterns in U.S. regions. Therefore, along with their greater leverage in Sunday talk shows and talk radio, conservatives use their advantage in print to create the distortion of liberal media bias, MMFA concludes.

As you read, consider the following questions:

1. Despite the decline in newspaper readership, why are newspapers still an important medium, in MMFA's view?

2. How does MMFA describe the top ten columnists?

3. How does MMFA support its claim that conservatives control newspapers across the United States?

This project did something that has never been done before: It amassed data on the syndicated columnists published by nearly every daily newspaper in the country. While a few publications, most notably *Editor & Publisher*, cover the syndicated newspaper industry, no one has attempted to comprehensively assemble this information prior to now. Because the syndicates refuse to reveal to the public exactly where their columnists are published, when *Media Matters for America* set out to make a systematic assessment of the syndicated columnist landscape, we had no choice but to contact each paper individually and ask which syndicated columnists are published on their op-ed pages.

The results show that in paper after paper, state after state, and region after region, conservative syndicated columnists get more space than their progressive counterparts. As *Editor & Publisher* paraphrased one syndicate executive noting, "U.S. dailies run more conservative than liberal columns, but some are willing to consider liberal voices." . . .

Though they have suffered slow but steady declines in readership over the last couple of decades, newspapers remain in many ways the most important of all news media. The Newspaper Association of America estimates that each copy of a weekday paper is read by an average of 2.1 adults, while each Sunday paper is read by an average of 2.5 adults, pushing total newspaper readership for daily papers to more than 116 million and Sunday papers to more than 134 million. This means that some columnists reach tens of millions of readers, and one, conservative George Will, actually reaches more than 50 million.

Furthermore, newspapers are the preferred news medium of those most interested in the news. According to a 2006 Pew Research Center study, 66 percent of those who say they follow political news closely regularly read newspapers, far more than the number who cite any other medium. And an almost identical proportion of those who say they "enjoy keeping up with the news"—more than half the population—turn to newspapers more than any other medium. These more aware citizens are in turn more likely to influence the opinions of their families, friends, and associates.

Syndicated newspaper columnists have a unique ability to influence public opinion and the national debate. And whether examining only the top columnists or the entire group, large papers or small, the data presented in this report make clear that conservative syndicated columnists enjoy a clear advantage over their progressive counterparts.

A Focus on Nationally Syndicated Columnists

By contacting newspapers directly, we were able to obtain information on the syndicated columnists run by 1,377 of the 1,430 English-language daily papers in the United States, or 96 percent.

We asked papers for two categories of syndicated columnists: those they publish regularly, meaning every week or almost every week: and those they publish occasionally, meaning at least once per month but not every week. Most of the analyses in this report are restricted to those columnists each paper publishes regularly, unless noted otherwise. . . .

[The study] focuses only on nationally syndicated columnists, not each paper's local columnists. It would have been impossible to determine the ideology of every one of the thousands of local columnists in the country, whereas the smaller number of syndicated columnists make them much easier to classify. In order to qualify, a columnist had to appear in three or more papers, and in papers in at least two states (there are many columnists who are syndicated to a few papers within one state; we established this rule to exclude those columnists). By this measure, there are 201 nationally syndicated columnists in America. In these raw numbers, the total list of columnists looks relatively balanced: there are 74 conservatives, 79 progressives, and 48 centrists.

That does not mean, however, that there is ideological balance among the nation's syndicated columnists. The truth is that conservatives have a clear and unmistakable advantage. Conservative columnists appear in more papers than progressive columnists do, and conservatives reach more readers. Most states find their newspapers' op-ed pages dominated by conservatives. In short, just as in so many other areas of the media, the right has the upper hand.

The Big Picture

If one were to throw a dart at a map of the United States and pick up the local newspaper where the dart landed, chances are one would be reading a paper whose op-ed pages lean to the right. Putting aside for a moment the question of circulation, the data show unequivocally that most newspapers in America run more conservative syndicated columnists than progressive columnists.

In fact, there are fully three newspapers that run more conservatives than progressives for every one newspaper that runs more progressives than conservatives.

While it might be easy to bring to mind a few prominent newspapers (e.g. *The New York Times*) that run more progressives, looking across the data it becomes clear that at every circulation level, one finds more papers that skew to the right on the op-ed pages. This difference is modest within the largest papers—the 103 papers with circulations over 100,000—but becomes an enormous gap that grows larger at each smaller level of circulation.

Obviously, larger newspapers tend to serve larger cities, which are not only more likely to have a progressive populace than smaller communities but also tend to be more demographically diverse in many ways. A small paper, on the other hand, may serve a local area that is relatively homogeneous. But without speculating too much about the ideological leanings of individual newspaper owners and the communities those papers serve, it can be said that smaller papers, at least on this measure, are more likely to lean right.

For instance, among the smallest daily newspapers—those with circulations under 10,000—64 percent run more regular conservative syndicated columnists than progressives, while only 16 percent run more progressives. Among papers with circulations between 10,000 and 25,000, the difference is similar: 62 percent run more conservatives, while only 18 percent run more progressives. Only among the largest papers were the two groups even somewhat close, with 50 percent running more conservatives and 35 percent running more progressives.

As interesting as these data are, they do not account completely for differences in the circulations of each paper. After all, the columnists printed in a paper with a circulation of 1 million will have greater impact than those printed in a paper with a circulation of 100,000. In order to more precisely account for circulation differences, we created a measure we call "relative ideological voice," which compares the reach and influence of columnists within a newspaper, within a state, or within the country as a whole. It multiplies the number of columnists of each ideological stripe by the circulation of the papers in which they appear.

Because conservative columnists have their greatest advantage in small papers, the imbalance in voice is not as great as the overall newspaper-by-newspaper advantage, wherein 60 percent of newspapers in the country run more conservatives and only 20 percent run more progressives. Nonetheless, conservatives retain a clear advantage over their progressive counterparts on a national level. When American newspaper readers turn to the op-ed page of their local newspaper each day, the syndicated columnists they see there are more likely to be conservative.

Top of the Charts

Every syndicated columnist holds a place within an elite stratum of our nation's political debate. But there are some who constitute the elite of the elite—and that group leans to the right.

Of the top ten columnists by number of papers, five are conservatives (George Will, Cal Thomas, Kathleen Parker, Morton Kondracke, and Thomas Sowell), two are centrists (David Broder and Cokie and Steve Roberts, who write a column together), and only three are progressives (Ellen Goodman, Leonard Pitts Jr., and Nat Hentoff). As the nation's most-read columnist, George Will appears in fully one out of every four daily newspapers in America.

When the data are sorted by the circulation of the papers that run each columnist, the same pattern emerges: five conservatives, two centrists, and three progressives. Though a few of the names have changed, once again, George Will is clearly at the head of the pack, reaching over 6 million more readers than his closest rival.

Overall, there are 79 progressives whose columns are regularly carried in multiple papers. These progressives appear regularly in a total of 1,915 papers (counting each paper as many times as it has columnists) with a summed circulation of 125.2 million. By comparison, there are 74 conservatives whose columns are regularly carried in multiple papers. These conservatives appear regularly in a total of 3,076 papers (counting each paper as many times as it has columnists) with a summed circulation of 152.1 million.

At the top, the disparity is just as stark. The top 10 conservative columnists appear in 641 more papers than the top 10 progressive columnists; the total circulation for the top 10 conservatives exceeds that of the top 10 progressives by more than 20 million readers.

It is worth noting that on both of these lists, there are columnists syndicated in relatively small numbers of papers. For instance, David Ignatius of *The Washington Post* is carried regularly in only 22 papers, but reaches more than 3.6 million readers. As such, he has the highest average circulation of any syndicated columnist. Others—Bob Herbert and Jonah Goldberg, for instance—also are published in mostly high-circulation papers.

At the other end of the scale are columnists who are published mostly in smaller papers. Progressive columnist Gene Lyons appears regularly in 75 papers, but they have an average circulation of less than 12,000, meaning he reaches less than a million readers.

As for centrist columnists, when one moves past the top two—David Broder and Thomas Friedman—there is a steep drop-off in the number of papers in which the columnists appear and the total circulation they reach.

If the large circulation numbers involved here are overwhelming, another way of thinking about the top columnists is their "reach"—how much of the American newspaper marketplace are they reaching? This can be expressed in percentage terms by dividing a columnist's total circulation with the total circulation of all daily newspapers in America, about 50 million. The fact that the combined circulation of the papers regularly carrying George Will is above 21 million means that he reaches two out of every five newspaper readers in America, an extraordinary level of penetration.

These elite columnists dominate the syndicated market-place to a dramatic degree. If we add up the combined circulation reached by all 201 syndicated columnists in this dataset, we see that the top 10 columnists alone account for more than 35 percent of the total syndicated market. The top 18 columnists reach as many readers as the other 183. George Will alone reaches as many readers as the bottom 80 columnists. The median columnist among the 201 in the dataset reaches 1 percent of the total American newspaper readership. In other words, this is an extraordinarily top-heavy list.

Conservative Advantage Across the Land

To this point, we have concerned ourselves with the national picture. But when one looks separately at regions and states, it becomes clear that the dominance of conservative syndicated columnists is spread across the nation. Once again, we are using the measure of relative ideological voice, the number of progressive, conservative, and centrist columns and how many readers they reach. We will start at the broadest level, then move closer to the ground.

It is often said that Americans are divided not only into red and blue states, but red and blue regions; the South and Midwest are more conservative, while the Northeast and West are more progressive. While most would agree that this is an oversimplified picture of Americans and their beliefs, we can say one thing about the broad regions of the country: In three of the four, conservatives have the advantage on the op-ed pages.

Due to the influence of the Middle Atlantic states—particularly New York, where progressives enjoy an advantage in some papers with very large circulations—progressives do manage to hold a slight edge (44 percent to 42 percent) in the Northeast. But in all three of the country's other large regions, conservative syndicated columnists reach more eyes more often than their progressive counterparts.

Furthermore, in every region of the country, the columnists appearing in the most papers are more likely to be conservative than progressive. Even in the Northeast, the region where progressives enjoy a small advantage in relative ideological voice, George Will appears in more papers than any other columnist. Will appears regularly in 63 papers in the Northeast, and occasionally in 8 more. The top 10 list for the Northeast shows five conservatives, four progressives, and one centrist.

The other region where progressives might hope to be at parity—the West—does show a slightly more balanced split among the top columnists. But here as well, George Will outranks all others, and the top 10 list includes more conservatives than progressives.

Given the extreme imbalance in relative ideological voice in the Midwest and South, it is no surprise that a similarly stark contrast emerges on the top 10 lists for those two regions.

In every region of the country, the columnist who appears in the most papers is a conservative: George Will in the Northeast and West, Kathleen Parker in the Midwest, and Cal Thomas in the South.

Next, using the nine areas into which the U.S. Census Bureau divides the country, the data show that in eight out of nine, the conservative voice outweighs the progressive voice.

The greatest advantage for conservatives—a margin of 50 percent to 33 percent (with centrists making up the remainder)—occurs in the South Atlantic, comprised of the Eastern Seaboard states running from Delaware south to Florida. Close behind, with a margin of 50 percent to 34 percent, is the West South Central, comprised of Texas, Oklahoma, Arkansas and Louisiana.

Only in the Middle Atlantic states—New York, Pennsylvania, and New Jersey—does the progressive voice loom larger than the conservative voice. Even in New England, the most progressive area of the country, conservative syndicated columnists have the advantage on the op-ed pages.

Finally, the relative balance of conservative and progressive syndicated columnists can be examined on the state level. Here, the data do not break down strictly on red-blue lines. There are some heavily Republican states where conservative columnists dominate as one might expect—South Carolina, Oklahoma, and Georgia, for example—and some heavily Democratic states where progressive columnists reach more readers. But there are also many "blue" states whose newspapers feature more conservative columnists. These include Illinois, Michigan, Connecticut, and California. Among the states where the progressive voice outweighs the conservative voice, there are Democratic states (Rhode Island, Vermont, Hawaii, New York) and swing states (Wisconsin, Arizona, and Tennessee), but no clearly "red" states.

But overall, the results are clear. Conservative syndicated columnists have a greater reach than their progressive columnists in 38 states, plus the District of Columbia. In only 12 states does the progressive voice outweigh the conservative voice.

Louder Than the Progressive Voice

Conservatives are often heard to complain about the "liberal media," a nefarious cabal of journalists and media owners supposedly endeavoring to twist the news to serve their ideological agenda. *Media Matters for America* has shown in a variety of ways that the "liberal media" is a myth. Our two reports on the Sunday talk shows showed how those programs are dominated by conservative guests. Our analysis of the coverage of religion showed how that coverage favors conservatives. Analyses performed by other organizations have shown how conservatives dominate talk radio. And this study demonstrates that in yet another key portion of the news media, conservatives enjoy a structural advantage that gives them a leg up in influencing public opinion.

That structural advantage enables them to transmit an overarching narrative across the country, one that serves to convey the impression that conservative ideas that in many cases enjoy tiny support are actually the "reasonable center" in key debates. To take just one example, prominent conservative columnists who wrote about the topic were nearly unanimous in support of President [George W.] Bush's decision to commute Scooter Libby's sentence, while some advocated pardoning him outright, despite the fact that polls indicated the decision had the support of only around one in five Americans.

In terms of the number of people reached by their ideas and opinions, of the authority they are granted, and of their prestige, there are few in the American news media who equal the lofty position held by the top syndicated columnists. Read by millions, even tens of millions, their opinions form the basis on which our democratic debate often proceeds. Because they have a national reach, they also have the power to advance ideas and narratives that local columnists simply do not have.

As this study has demonstrated, the landscape of syndicated columnists is dominated by conservatives. They reach considerably more readers than progressives. By a 3-to-1 margin, most American newspapers run more conservative syndicated columnists than progressives. In nearly every region of the country, the conservative voice on op-ed pages is louder than the progressive voice. And for every one state that has a greater progressive voice, there are three in which conservatives have more influence.

In short, while the right wing spends a great deal of time complaining about alleged bias in the media, when it comes to the nation's op-ed pages, it is the progressives who are getting the short end of the stick.

| *"Journalists who think they know com-
munities of color end up writing stereotypical stories."*

Racism and Ethnic Bias in the Media Is a Serious Problem

Lena-Snomeka Gomes

In the following viewpoint from her interview with Lena-Snomeka Gomes, Elizabeth Llorente states that unequal and inaccurate representations of minorities still persist in the media, and media professionals who are minorities continue to face prejudice in the industry. In Llorente's view, reporters of color often feel unwelcome when entering white communities. In addition, she claims other journalists continue to draw upon harmful ethnic and religious stereotypes. Diversity and opportunities for minorities in newsrooms also are lacking, she contends, compounding these problems. Llorente is an award-winning senior reporter for The Record *in Bergen, New Jersey. A former newswriter, Gomes is a program support specialist at the Homeless Children's Network in San Francisco.*

Lena-Snomeka Gomes, "We Can Do It Better: Award-winning journalist Elizabeth Llorente discusses the nuances of reporting on race and ethnicity," Center for Integration and Improvement of Journalism, July 8, 2004. Reproduced by permission.

As you read, consider the following questions:

1. According to Llorente, why is covering one's own ethnic community not necessarily easier?

2. What barriers do reporters face when reporting on immigrants, in the author's view?

3. Why are there still very few minorities in newsrooms, in Llorente's opinion?

Elizabeth Llorente, senior reporter for *The Record* in Bergen, New Jersey, was recently honored with the Career Achievement Award from the Let's Do It Better Workshop on Race and Ethnicity at the Columbia University Graduate School of Journalism. Llorente was honored for her more than 10 years of reporting on the nation's changing demographics. Her series, "Diverse and Divided," documented the racial tensions and political struggles between Hispanic immigrants and African Americans in Patterson, N.J. Llorente spoke with *NewsWatch* about the nuances of reporting on race and ethnicity.

Lena-Snomeka Gomes: What are some of the major barriers journalists face, especially journalists of color when writing about race and ethnicity?

Elizabeth Llorente: Well it depends on what they look like. For example, I know that some of the African American reporters that I have worked with have spoken about feelings of being unwelcome, especially when they're covering white areas. And there are also other reporters who feel different because they stand out from the time they walk into a room. People make assumptions about them. I have been told that it's hard to tell what my race is. Is this positive or negative? Maybe it helps when I'm doing a story about tension and whites are part of the tension. Sometimes, I suspect, they open up more because they don't know that I am Hispanic. Perhaps, they would not have been as candid had they known.

However, it's not necessarily easier to cover stories in your own ethnic community or communities similar to yours. If you criticize people and they didn't like it, they are usually less forgiving. They take it personal and see you as a traitor, especially when the stories involve a politically charged group.

Do you think journalists of color are resistant to writing about race and ethnicity because they don't want to be typecast so to speak?

There are people who believe that and I don't blame them. Sometimes that's all the papers will let them do, and the papers don't value their work. In that regard, it's a thankless job. When you come back with a great story, they don't see the skill and the talent it took to report and write that story. They think, of course, you wrote well because you're one of them. They automatically assume it was easy for you to get the story. They may even question your objectivity. But, when [Pulitzer Prize-winning journalist] Rick Bragg went to the South to write about the life he knew, no one said, of course its easy for him because he's from the South. No, they said, wow he's a great writer.

Do you think stories about race and ethnicity still face being calendared for special events or has there been more sustained coverage and focus?

It's gotten much better. Stories used to be covered for Black History Month or Cinco de Mayo, but now beats have been created around race and ethnicity. Beat reporters have to write all year. Reporters are interested in writing about race and ethnicity. They want to cover these issues. Now the next level journalism needs to go to is to spread the responsibility of covering race and ethnicity among all reporters, in all sections of the paper, business section, education, transportation, and municipal. Coverage has to be more comprehensive. It cannot be reserved for certain reporters, because race and ethnicity is such a huge area.

Minority-owned Stations and TV Households

- Minority-owned stations reach 22 percent of all U.S. TV households and just 30 percent of all minority U.S. TV households.

- Hispanic- or Latino-owned stations reach just 21.7 percent of the Latino TV households in the United States.

- Black- or African American-owned stations reach just 5.3 percent of the African American TV households in the United States.

- Asian-owned stations reach just 24 percent of the Asian TV households in the United States.

- Over 10 percent of the nation's Hispanic or Latino TV homes are in the New York City market, where there are no Latino-owned stations.

S. Derek Turner, "Out of the Picture 2007: Minority and Female TV Station Ownership in the United States," Free Press, October 2007. www.freepress.net.

Immigration Stories

How do stories about immigration differ from other stories about race and ethnicity?

If you're writing about second or third generation Cubans, you're writing about Americans, a minority group that has some stake here. With immigrants, you're writing about people who are newer, who don't necessarily feel American. They are still transitioning into this national culture. They are rebuilding their identities. For example, they may not have a sense of (their) civil rights here or of American racism.

What skills do journalists have to master in order to report fairly and accurately on immigrant communities?

First of all, you need to have a completely open mind. This is especially important when you're covering immigrant communities. So many of us think that we know the immigrant groups, but many of us only know the stereotypes. Too often we set out to write stories that end up marginalizing people in harmful ways because the stories tend to exacerbate those stereotypes. Or we ignore the stories that do not conform to the stereotypes. For example, if we're going to write about Hispanic communities, instead of looking for Hispanics in the suburbs, we tend to go where we can most readily find them, in Miami, Spanish Harlem, and in the Barrio. We keep telling the same stories and giving it the same frame, because it's an easy thing to do when you're on a deadline. The result is an ok story. But immigration stories are diverse. They are not only in enclaves, but also in places we never thought about finding them in, such as in once exclusively white suburbs and rural America. Perhaps Hispanics in the barrio is a valuable story, but that is no longer the Hispanic story. It is a Hispanic story.

Okay, once you find (immigrant communities) how do you communicate with them?

It's tough. Not knowing the language can be difficult. But the key is to start out with the attitude of not settling for less. Start out speaking with the leaders, but only as a vehicle to reach the other people who are not always in the papers. Too many of us stop with the leaders and that is not enough. Ask them to introduce you or ask them if you can use their name to open up a few doors for you to speak with others in the community. However, covering immigrant communities doesn't mean encountering a language barrier. Many people have a basic knowledge of English. You can still conduct an interview with someone who only speaks survival English. But, you will also run into a lot of people who don't speak

English. If you make the effort, if you're patient, if you speak slower and are conscious of the words you use, if you make sure they understand what you are asking them, if you tune in, you'll make the connection. Finally, if language is a barrier and you're not comfortable, find someone who is bilingual to help you interpret.

How can journalists write balanced stories if they operate from the stereotypes?

Ask the person you're interviewing to break down those stereotypes. You can tell the person that there is a particular stereotype and ask them if it is true or not. Journalists have the unique role and power to help break the stereotypes down.

What does receiving the Career Achievement Award mean to you?

I was hoping that it would mean that I could retire and go sailing and write my novels from a log cabin. After I checked my retirement savings, I realized, that ain't gonna happen for a long time. Its nice to get awards, but when you get one it's usually for a certain story or project. This is like a wonderful embrace that says, you know, you hit the ball out of the park again and again. You set a standard in this business. At a career level, you have done great work. It's just a nice sweeping kiss and hug to me.

The Culture of Journalism

Tell me some of the successes Let's Do It Better has had and some of the ways in which it has impacted the culture of journalism.

I think one wonderful thing they did, under Sig Gissler (original founder), was that they targeted the gatekeepers. His model approach was to go directly to the top management. Gissler wanted to show them good reporting that reached a higher level and how stories about race were more nuanced.

He wanted them to read the stories and then to talk to the folks who wrote them so they could learn how to do these types of stories.

Did the top respond?

Yes! I saw conversions. People who started out cynically were changed by the last day. They were beginning to look at race and ethnicity stories critically. They were going to raise their standard. They left the workshops believing that their news organizations needed more diverse voices.

Why, are there still so few people of color in newsrooms today?

Too many employers are prejudiced. Too many minorities are still being hired under a cloud of doubt. I don't think many minorities are hired with the notion that they will be star reporters. They are not nurtured. Then when minority journalists leave it's seen as a betrayal, but when whites leave, it's considered a good career move. I have worked with many white reporters who have had many opportunities in training and promotions, and nobody says they're ungrateful s.o.b.'s when they leave.

Can we keep doing it better?

Of course. There are still so many stories we are not getting that are out there. Journalists who think they know communities of color end up writing stereotypical stories and they use photos to make people look exotic. In fact, we need to pay more attention to photojournalism. A story can be fair and balanced, but if that picture projects the exotic stereotype, the story loses its value. Don't bypass a photo of a person because they don't look 'ethnic enough.' Take a picture of the blonde Mexican or the Muslim women wearing Levi jeans.

"The media establishment is convinced that pervasive and profound racism is unique to whites and, therefore, downplays and apologizes for manifestations of racial hatred among non-whites."

Racism and Bias Against Ethnic Groups in the Media Is Not a Problem

Ian Jobling

Ian Jobling owns and writes the content for White America *(Formerly* The Inverted World*), a racialist Web site, and is a former writer for* American Renaissance, *a racialist magazine. In the following viewpoint, Jobling argues that the "political correctness" of mainstream media perpetuates unfounded allegations of white racism. The author proposes that hate crimes have been fabricated and major news outlets malign journalists and experts who critique black failings and culture. Ultimately, Jobling believes that liberal biases in news coverage downplay anti-white prejudices among ethnic groups, further fueling the belief that white racism is the root of minorities' problems and shortcomings.*

Ian Jobling, "Liberal Media Bias and the Myth of White Racism," *White America*, August 15, 2008. Reproduced by permission.

As you read, consider the following questions:

1. How does Jobling support his claim that a 1996 black church burning was a hoax?

2. According to Jobling, how have works and arguments critiquing blacks been described by the media?

3. How does the author support his assertion that mass media ignore minorities' racist attitudes towards whites?

Several *White America* articles have dealt with anti-white, or "leukophobic," bias in the media. However, a comprehensive perspective on liberal media bias on race has been lacking. Fortunately, William McGowan's *Coloring the News: How Crusading for Diversity Has Corrupted American Journalism*, by far the most penetrating and thorough treatment of liberal bias in the news media, provides the basis for such a perspective. Since the book was published in 2001, McGowan's examples are now dated, but media bias is plainly as egregious today as it was in the 1990s, as examinations of the coverage of the Duke lacrosse rape scandal and the Jena Six case will show.

McGowan paints a portrait of a media establishment that obsessively promulgates what I will call "the myth of white racism" at the expense of objectivity and accuracy. According to the myth, irrational hatred and fear of non-whites is rampant among white Americans and causes whites to subject non-whites to discrimination and abuse. To bolster this myth, the media establishment eagerly seeks out incidents that reveal white racism. This eagerness often causes journalists to fall for hoaxes and poorly supported accusations of racist treatment. The media establishment also believes that white racism is the primary reason for high rates of poverty, incarceration, and other types of social dysfunction among non-whites. Consequently, the establishment censors and silences journalists who suggest non-whites themselves might be responsible for their failings. Finally, the media establishment is convinced that pervasive and profound racism is unique to whites and, therefore, downplays and apologizes for manifestations of racial hatred among non-whites.

McGowan gives several examples of incidents in which the press, eager to expose white racism, leapt to conclusions that were later proved false. The most flagrant is the 1996 black church burning hysteria. The story began with a report from Center for Democratic Renewal, a leftist activist group, that claimed there had been a surge in arson attacks against black churches in the South. The attacks were supposedly perpetrated by "night riders," recruited from among the ranks of white supremacist groups like the KKK and the Aryan Brotherhood.

The story appealed so deeply to journalists' stereotypes about race that the church burnings became one of the major stories of the year, generating over 2200 newspaper articles. Earnest editorialists scorched readers with the full heat of their liberal outrage. *USA Today* said the fires were an "attempt to murder the spirit of black America." The *New York Times* called the attacks an "epidemic of racial terror." The media establishment interpreted the burnings as a manifestation of widespread anti-black racial hatred among whites. As Jack White of *Time* fumed, "the coded phrases" of Republican leaders "who build their careers George Wallace-style on a foundation of race-baiting" were "encouraging the arsonists." *New York Times* columnist Bob Herbert wrote, "The fuel for these fires can be traced to a carefully crafted environment of bigotry and hatred that was developed over the past quarter century."

After all of this, investigations finally revealed that the whole story was false and perhaps even a deliberate hoax. There had been no increase in church burnings in recent years—there had, in fact, been a decline. Arsonists burned down more white churches than black ones. An investigation by the Alabama government found not a single instance of racial motivation in arson attacks on churches in the state, and such attacks were also extremely rare elsewhere. The media had been led astray by its eagerness to crusade against white racism.[1]

The second prejudice that slants media coverage of race is that white racism is the primary explanation for the failings of non-whites, such as high rates of incarceration and illegitimacy. The press has cast the war on drugs as a war on blacks that unfairly sentences them to illegitimate hardship. In 1996, *Washington Post* writer Courtland Millroy attacked three-strikes laws that sentence repeat offenders to long prison sentences as a manifestation of white hostility to blacks: "If you were writing a law to target blacks one could scarcely have done it more effectively than three strikes." McGowan also cites evidence that the press ignores research that argues there is no racial bias in the criminal justice system.[2] Similarly, a Newsday columnist named Les Payne improbably blamed the high black illegitimacy rate on the legacy of slavery, when slaves were deprived of the legal right to marry and forced to bear children out of wedlock.[3]

The media establishment tends to be hostile to work that threatens the dogma that white racism is responsible for black failings. Thus, Dinesh D'Souza's 1995 book *The End of Racism*, which argued that black poverty was blacks' own fault, was greeted with hysterical and unfair abuse from a *Time* magazine reviewer, who said it was "full of obscene ideas" and proved that "bigotry sells books."[4]

This hostility was particularly evident in the reaction to Eugene Richards' 1994 *Cocaine True, Cocaine Blue*, a photojournalistic depiction of drug addiction in America's inner cities. The book contained disturbing images of the reality of the black underclass, including a photo of a deranged-looking woman clenching a syringe in her nearly toothless mouth, as well as interviews with drug addicts and dealers. In the *New*

York Times Book Review, Brent Staples accused Richards of staging the photos to make blacks look bad and whined, "Couldn't Mr. Richards have found a setting where most or at least half of the drug addicts are white?"[5]

Sometimes journalists disguise the embarrassing reality of black failure by glamorizing it. In 1996, the *New York Times* ran a profile of rap producer Suge Knight, who had a long criminal record and collaborated with the most violent, antisocial "gansta rappers." The piece recognized Knight's vile past, yet managed to transmute him into a sort of rebel hero. Knight and his associates:

> move at their own time, they do things their own way. Suge and his boys are grand. Men without women, they believe the masculine code defines everything.[6]

The last component of the myth is the conviction that pervasive and profound racism is unique to whites. This prejudice causes journalists to hide or downplay racial hatred among non-whites. In their coverage of Louis Farrakhan's 1995 Million Man March, the press soft-pedaled Farrakhan's history of anti-white hate mongering, which included accusing the US government of inventing the AIDS virus as a means of genocide against blacks. Rather, reporters did their best to paint the event in a positive light. One *Washington Post* reporter was "overcome . . . with the sights, sounds and spirit of a community renewing itself in a day-long myth-shattering celebration of smiling faces, slapping hands, upbeat voices, hugs and goodwill." Reporters emphasized the lip-service to tolerance and downplayed the race-baiting and zany conspiracy theories in Farrakhan's speech at the march.[7]

Two more recent incidents confirm that the media bias McGowan identifies is still present, and probably even more virulent, today. In the notorious Duke [University, N.C.] lacrosse rape case of 2006, the media were once again tripped up by their eagerness to promote the myth of white racism.

"Valuing Differences"

Ignore the smoke screen platitudes about "valuing differences." Unity demands unanimity. If you don't accept the left-leaning agenda of advocacy journalism, you're enabling racism. If you don't support the pursuit of racial hiring goals as a primary journalistic goal, you're selling out. If you don't buy the idea that a first-generation Filipina should feel ethnic solidarity with a fourth-generation Japanese-American simply because they share the same hair and eye color, you're denying your "identity."

Michelle Malkin,
"Journalists' Group-think Is Not Unity,"
Jewish World Review, *July 14, 1999.*
www.jewishworldreview.com.

The incident began in March when black stripper and prostitute Crystal Mangum accused members of the Duke lacrosse team of having raped her at a party where she had been hired to perform. Despite the lack of evidence for Mangum's claim, and much evidence contradicting it, District Attorney Mike Nifong aggressively prosecuted and publicized the alleged crime. The media collaborated in this smear of the students, granting Nifong dozens of sympathetic interviews during which he painted a ghastly portrait of what he called "ganglike rape activity accompanied by the racial slurs and general racial hostility."[8] Over the coming months, the case became a *cause célèbre*, just as the church burnings had a decade before. Editorialists fumed with outrage. For example, in "Bonded in Barbarity," *New York Times* columnist Selena Roberts railed against "a group of privileged players of fine pedigree entangled in a night that threatens to belie their social standing as human beings."[9] Nancy Grace of CNN assumed the players were guilty, dismissed all evidence to the contrary, and subjected the players to insults. "The Blue Devils!" she said, "It may not be just a nickname at Duke University."[10]

After nearly a year of hysteria, the case against the players unraveled, and they were found innocent of all charges. In the aftermath, some press commentators admitted that they and their colleagues had taken the stance they did because the story appealed to their prejudices. As a reporter from the Raleigh *News & Observer*, reflected, "I was viewing the scenario through the prism of white liberal guilt. . . . I stereotyped the entire Duke lacrosse team."[11]

Despite this soul searching, the next year proved that journalists had not learned a thing. This time the source of outrage was the allegation that white high school students in Jena, Louisiana had displayed racial hatred towards blacks and that blacks were treated in an unfair manner by the criminal justice system. The media's story, which was again taken uncritically from the account of a leftist activist group, went as follows. On August 31 [2007], the white students had hung nooses from a tree on Jena High School grounds in order to mark it as a "whites-only tree" that blacks were forbidden to sit under. Three months later, a group of black students who became known as the "Jena Six," retaliating for the noose incident and other alleged racist treatment, attacked a white student named Justin Barker, who was not one of the students responsible for the nooses. In what seemed like a clear instance of disparate treatment by race, five of the black students were initially charged with attempted murder in the courts, whereas the white students had only gotten nine-day suspensions from the school board for the noose incident.

Typical of the furious tone the media adopted in covering the story was the *New York Post*'s description of the noose-hanging incident as a throwback to "the reign of lynching terror that once permeated the South." Thanks in large part to the investigations of Craig Franklin, an assistant editor at *The Jena Times*, the whole story was revealed as a patchwork of falsehoods. There had never been any "whites-only tree" at the high school. A black student had jokingly suggested that the tree might be reserved for whites the day before the noose incident, but everyone at the school understood the joke for what it was. The nooses were not intended as a reference to the South's history of lynching. Rather, the students had gotten the idea of nooses from the *Lonesome Dove*, a television show set in the Old West that depicted lynchings of cattle rustlers. The prank was directed at the students' white friends on the school's rodeo team, not at blacks. There was no evidence that the attack on Barker was related to the noose incident either; such a link had not been suggested by anyone interviewed during investigations of the attack. As Franklin concluded:

> I have never before witnessed such a disgrace in professional journalism. Myths replaced facts, and journalists abdicated their solemn duty to investigate every claim because they were seduced by a powerfully appealing but false narrative of racial injustice.

Finally, the initial charge of attempted murder, which was later dropped, against the black students was not a clear case of racial injustice, as the attack on Barker was severe enough to endanger his life. Mychal Bell, one of the Jena Six, had knocked Barker unconscious by slamming his head against a concrete beam, after which the gang had stomped and kicked him. Bell had four prior convictions for crimes of violence. By casting the attack as a response to racism followed by unjust sentencing, the media perpetuated the myth that whites are to blame for high black crime and incarceration rates.

Coloring the News is an indispensable book for anyone who is interested in any aspect of liberal bias or "political correctness" in the media—McGowan also deals with the coverage of women's issues, homosexuality, and immigration. His work on race paints a comprehensive portrait of the stubborn prejudices that slant news coverage. Unfortunately, McGowan's book has not prevented the media from making the mistakes he skewered over and over again.

Notes

1. William McGowan, *Coloring the News: How Crusading for Diversity Has Corrupted American Journalism* (San Francisco: Encounter Books, 2001), 88–94.
2. Ibid., 75.
3. Ibid., 43.
4. Ibid., 42.
5. Ibid., 47.
6. Ibid., 51.
7. Ibid., 71.
8. Stuart Taylor, Jr. and K.C. Johnson, *Until Proven Innocent: Political Correctness and the Shameful Injustices of the Duke Lacrosse Rape Case* (New York: Thomas Dunne, 2007), 87.
9. Ibid., 121.
10. Ibid., 124.
11. Ibid., 125.

"*For citizens who value media democracy and the public interest, broadcast regulation of our publicly owned airwaves has reached a low-water mark.*"

Broadcasters Should Be Required to Air a Variety of Opposing Views

Steve Rendall

The Fairness Doctrine, which was effective between 1949 and 1987, required licensed television and radio broadcasters to provide contrasting views while covering controversial topics. In the following viewpoint, Steve Rendall asserts that the abolishment of the doctrine has resulted in less substantial and unbalanced coverage of important issues in the media. He proposes that misconceptions about the law ultimately led to its demise at the hands of anti-regulation Republicans. As a result, the author insists conservatives have come to dominate the airwaves with their partisan views, which he believes underscores the importance of the Fairness Doctrine. Rendall is a senior analyst for FAIR (Fairness & Accuracy in Reporting), a national media watch group.

Steve Rendall, "The Fairness Doctrine: How We Lost It, and Why We Need It Back," *Extra!*, January–February 2005. Reproduced by permission.

As you read, consider the following questions:

1. What misconceptions existed about the Fairness Doctrine, as stated by the author?

2. In Rendall's view, how was the Fairness Doctrine abolished?

3. What examples does Rendall provide to support his allegation that conservatives currently control broadcast communications?

A license permits broadcasting, but the licensee has no constitutional right to be the one who holds the license or to monopolize a . . . frequency to the exclusion of his fellow citizens. There is nothing in the First Amendment which prevents the Government from requiring a licensee to share his frequency with others. . . . It is the right of the viewers and listeners, not the right of the broadcasters, which is paramount.

—*U.S. Supreme Court, upholding the constitutionality of the Fairness Doctrine in Red Lion Broadcasting Co. v. FCC, 1969.*

When the Sinclair Broadcast Group retreated from preelection plans [in October 2004] to force its 62 television stations to preempt prime-time programming in favor of airing the blatantly anti-John Kerry [former Democratic presidential nominee] documentary *Stolen Honor: Wounds that Never Heal*, the reversal wasn't triggered by a concern for fairness: Sinclair backpedaled because its stock was tanking. The staunchly conservative broadcaster's plan had provoked calls for sponsor boycotts, and Wall Street saw a company that was putting politics ahead of profits. Sinclair's stock declined by nearly 17 percent before the company announced it would air a somewhat more balanced news program in place of the documentary.

But if fairness mattered little to Sinclair, the news that a corporation that controlled more TV licenses than any other could put the publicly owned airwaves to partisan use sparked discussion of fairness across the board, from media democracy activists to television industry executives.

Variety underlined industry concerns in a [October 25, 2004] report suggesting that Sinclair's partisanship was making other broadcasters nervous by fueling "anti-consolidation forces" and efforts to bring back the FCC's [Federal Communications Commission] defunct Fairness Doctrine:

> Sinclair could even put the Fairness Doctrine back in play, a rule established in 1949 to require that the networks—all three of them—air all sides of issues. The doctrine was abandoned in the 1980s with the proliferation of cable, leaving citizens with little recourse over broadcasters that misuse the public airwaves, except to oppose the renewal of licenses.

The Sinclair controversy brought discussion of the Fairness Doctrine back to news columns and opinion pages cross the country. *Legal Times* weighed in with an in-depth essay headlined: "A Question of Fair Air Play: Can Current Remedies for Media Bias Handle Threats Like Sinclair's Aborted Anti-Kerry Program?"

Sinclair's history of one-sided editorializing and right-wing water-carrying, which long preceded its *Stolen Honor* ploy, puts it in the company of political talk radio, where right-wing opinion is the rule, locally and nationally. Together, they are part of a growing trend that sees movement conservatives and Republican partisans using the publicly owned airwaves as a political megaphone—one that goes largely unanswered by any regular opposing perspective. It's an imbalance that begs for a remedy.

A Short History of Fairness

The necessity for the Fairness Doctrine, according to proponents, arises from the fact that there are many fewer broadcast licenses than people who would like to have them. Unlike publishing, where the tools of the trade are in more or less endless supply, broadcasting licenses are limited by the finite number of available frequencies. Thus, as trustees of a scarce public resource, licensees accept certain public interest obligations in exchange for the exclusive use of limited public airwaves. One such obligation was the Fairness Doctrine, which was meant to ensure that a variety of views, beyond those of the licensees and those they favored, were heard on the airwaves. (Since cable's infrastructure is privately owned and cable channels can, in theory, be endlessly multiplied, the FCC does not put public interest requirements on that medium.)

The Fairness Doctrine had two basic elements: It required broadcasters to devote some of their airtime to discussing controversial matters of public interest, and to air contrasting views regarding those matters. Stations were given wide latitude as to how to provide contrasting views: It could be done through news segments, public affairs shows or editorials.

Formally adopted as an FCC rule in 1949 and repealed in 1987 by Ronald Reagan's pro-broadcaster FCC, the doctrine can be traced back to the early days of broadcast regulation.

Early on, legislators wrestled over competing visions of the future of radio: Should it be commercial or non-commercial? There was even a proposal by the U.S. Navy to control the new technology. The debate included early arguments about how to address the public interest, as well as fears about the awesome power conferred on a handful of licensees.

> American thought and American politics will be largely at the mercy of those who operate these stations, for publicity is the most powerful weapon that can be wielded in a republic. And when such a weapon is placed in the hands of one person, or a single selfish group is permitted to either tacitly or otherwise acquire ownership or dominate these broadcasting stations throughout the country, then woe be

to those who dare to differ with them. It will be impossible to compete with them in reaching the ears of the American people.

—*Rep. Luther Johnson (D.-Texas),*
in the debate that preceded the Radio Act of 1927.

In the Radio Act of 1927, Congress mandated the FCC's forerunner, the Federal Radio Commission (FRC), to grant broadcasting licenses in such a manner as to ensure that licensees served the "public convenience, interest or necessity."

As former FCC commissioner Nicholas Johnson pointed out, it was in that spirit that the FRC, in 1928, first gave words to a policy formulation that would become known as the Fairness Doctrine, calling for broadcasters to show "due regard for the opinions of others." In 1949, the FCC adopted the doctrine as a formal rule (FCC, Report on Editorializing by Broadcast Licensees, 1949).

In 1959 Congress amended the Communications Act of 1934 to enshrine the Fairness Doctrine into law, rewriting Chapter 315(a) to read: "A broadcast licensee shall afford reasonable opportunity for discussion of conflicting views on matters of public importance."

It is the purpose of the First Amendment to preserve an uninhibited marketplace of ideas in which truth will ultimately prevail, rather than to countenance monopolization of that market, whether it be by the government itself or a private licensee. It is the right of the public to receive suitable access to social, political, esthetic, moral and other ideas and experiences which is crucial here. That right may not constitutionally be abridged either by Congress or by the FCC.

—*U.S. Supreme Court,*
Red Lion Broadcasting Co. v. FCC, 1969.

A decade later the United States Supreme Court upheld the doctrine's constitutionality in *Red Lion Broadcasting Co. v. FCC* (1969), foreshadowing a decade in which the FCC would view the Fairness Doctrine as a guiding principle, calling it "the single most important requirement of operation in the public interest—the sine qua non for grant of a renewal of license" (FCC Fairness Report, 1974).

How It Worked

There are many misconceptions about the Fairness Doctrine. For instance, it did not require that each program be internally balanced, nor did it mandate equal time for opposing points of view. And it didn't require that the balance of a station's program lineup be anything like 50/50.

Nor, as [conservative talk radio show host] Rush Limbaugh has repeatedly claimed, was the Fairness Doctrine all that stood between conservative talkshow hosts and the dominance they would attain after the doctrine's repeal. In fact, not one Fairness Doctrine decision issued by the FCC had ever concerned itself with talkshows. Indeed, the talkshow format was born and flourished while the doctrine was in operation. Before the doctrine was repealed, right-wing hosts frequently dominated talkshow schedules, even in liberal cities, but none was ever muzzled. The Fairness Doctrine simply prohibited stations from broadcasting from a single perspective, day after day, without presenting opposing views.

In answer to charges, put forward in the *Red Lion* case, that the doctrine violated broadcasters' First Amendment free speech rights because the government was exerting editorial control, Supreme Court Justice Byron White wrote: "There is no sanctuary in the First Amendment for unlimited private censorship operating in a medium not open to all." In a [1994] *Washington Post* column, the Media Access Project (MAP), a telecommunications law firm that supports the Fairness Doctrine, addressed the First Amendment issue: "The Supreme

Bringing More Voices into the Marketplace of Ideas

In operation, the fairness doctrine has fulfilled the objectives of the First Amendment by bringing more voices into the marketplace of ideas, thereby maximizing the discussion of issues in our democracy. This extraordinarily difficult accomplishment has been achieved through a largely self-enforcing administrative mechanism that minimally intrudes into the editorial processes of the broadcaster. The fairness doctrine has had virtually no day-to-day impact on the operations of broadcast licensees, affording significant protection at almost no cost.

By emphasizing citizen-broadcaster conciliation as a prerequisite to any FCC [Federal Communications Commission] involvement, the fairness doctrine as administered has actually restricted direct governmental interference in the operations of broadcast licenses. It has also encouraged the development of ongoing relationships between broadcasters and members of their community of service, helping to create a forum that actually prevents misunderstandings and eliminates disputes before they arise.

Gigi B. Sohn,
"Is a Fairness Doctrine Needed Today?
Let's Restore Fairness to Broadcasting,"
World & I, *January 1994.*

ourt unanimously found [the Fairness Doctrine] advances First Amendment values. It safeguards the public's right to be informed on issues affecting our democracy, while also balancing broadcasters' rights to the broadest possible editorial discretion."

Indeed, when it was in place, citizen groups used the Fairness Doctrine as a tool to expand speech and debate. For instance, it prevented stations from allowing only one side to be heard on ballot measures. Over the years, it had been supported by grassroots groups across the political spectrum, including the ACLU [American Civil Liberties Union], National Rifle Association and the right-wing Accuracy In Media.

Typically, when an individual or citizens group complained to a station about imbalance, the station would set aside time for an on-air response for the omitted perspective: "Reasonable opportunity for presentation of opposing points of view," was the relevant phrase. If a station disagreed with the complaint, feeling that an adequate range of views had already been presented, the decision would be appealed to the FCC for a judgment.

According to Andrew Jay Schwartzman, president of MAP, scheduling response time was based on time of day, frequency and duration of the original perspective. "If one view received a lot of coverage in primetime," Schwartzman told *Extra!*, "then at least some response time would have to be in primetime. Likewise if one side received many short spots or really long spots." But the remedy did not amount to equal time; the ratio of airtime between the original perspective and the response "could be as much as five to one," said Schwartzman.

As a guarantor of balance and inclusion, the Fairness Doctrine was no panacea. It was somewhat vague, and depended on the vigilance of listeners and viewers to notice imbalance. But its value, beyond the occasional remedies it provided, was in its codification of the principle that broadcasters had a responsibility to present a range of views on controversial issues.

The Doctrine's Demise

From the 1920s through the '70s, the history of the Fairness Doctrine paints a picture of public servants wrestling with how to maintain some public interest standards in the operation of publicly owned—but corporate-dominated—airwaves. Things were about to change.

The 1980s brought the Reagan Revolution, with its army of anti-regulatory extremists; not least among these was [President Ronald] Reagan's new FCC chair, Mark S. Fowler. Formerly a broadcast industry lawyer, Fowler earned his reputation as "the James Watt [Scottish inventor of the practical steam engine, which ushered in the Industrial Revolution] of the FCC" by sneering at the notion that broadcasters had a unique role or bore special responsibilities to ensure democratic discourse. It was all nonsense, said Fowler: "The perception of broadcasters as community trustees should be replaced by a view of broadcasters as marketplace participants." To Fowler, television was "just another appliance—it's a toaster with pictures," and he seemed to endorse total deregulation: "We've got to look beyond the conventional wisdom that we must somehow regulate this box."

Of course, Fowler and associates didn't favor total deregulation: Without licensing, the airwaves would descend into chaos as many broadcasters competed for the same frequencies, a situation that would mean ruin for the traditional corporate broadcasters they were so close to. But regulation for the public good rather than corporate convenience was deemed suspect.

Fowler vowed to see the Fairness Doctrine repealed, and though he would depart the commission a few months before the goal was realized, he worked assiduously at setting the stage for the doctrine's demise.

He and his like-minded commissioners, a majority of whom had been appointed by President Ronald Reagan, argued that the doctrine violated broadcasters First Amendment free speech rights by giving government a measure of editorial control over stations. Moreover, rather than increase debate and discussion of controversial issues, they argued, the doctrine actually chilled debate, because stations feared demands for response time and possible challenges to broadcast licenses (though only one license was ever revoked in a dispute involving the Fairness Doctrine).

The FCC stopped enforcing the doctrine in the mid-'80s, well before it formally revoked it. As much as the commission majority wanted to repeal the doctrine outright, there was one hurdle that stood between them and their goal: Congress' 1959 amendment to the Communications Act had made the doctrine law.

Help would come in the form of a controversial 1986 legal decision by Judge Robert Bork and then-Judge Antonin Scalia, both Reagan appointees on the D.C. Circuit of the U.S. Court of Appeals. Their 2-1 opinion avoided the constitutional issue altogether, and simply declared that Congress had not actually made the doctrine into a law. Wrote Bork: "We do not believe that language adopted in 1959 made the Fairness Doctrine a binding statutory obligation," because, he said, the doctrine was imposed "under," not "by" the Communications Act of 1934. Bork held that the 1959 amendment established that the FCC could apply the doctrine, but was not obliged to do so— that keeping the rule or scuttling it was simply a matter of FCC discretion.

"The decision contravened 25 years of FCC holdings that the doctrine had been put into law in 1959," according to MAP. But it signaled the end of the Fairness Doctrine, which was repealed in 1987 by the FCC under new chair Dennis R. Patrick, a lawyer and Reagan White House aide.

A year after the doctrine's repeal, writing in *California Lawyer*, former FCC commissioner Johnson summed up the fight to bring back the Fairness Doctrine as "a struggle for nothing less than possession of the First Amendment: Who gets to have and express opinions in America." Though a bill before Congress to reinstate the doctrine passed overwhelmingly later that year, it failed to override Reagan's veto. Another attempt to resurrect the doctrine in 1991 ran out of steam when President George H.W. Bush threatened another veto.

Where Things Stand

What has changed since the repeal of the Fairness Doctrine? Is there more coverage of controversial issues of public importance? "Since the demise of the Fairness Doctrine we have had much less coverage of issues," says MAP's Schwartzman, adding that television news and public affairs programming has decreased locally and nationally. According to a study conducted by MAP and the Benton Foundation, 25 percent of broadcast stations no longer offer any local news or public affairs programming at all.

The most extreme change has been in the immense volume of unanswered conservative opinion heard on the airwaves, especially on talk radio. Nationally, virtually all of the leading political talkshow hosts are right-wingers: Rush Limbaugh, Sean Hannity, Michael Savage, Oliver North, G. Gordon Liddy, Bill O'Reilly and Michael Reagan, to name just a few. The same goes for local talkshows. One product of the post-Fairness era is the conservative "Hot Talk" format, featuring one right-wing host after another and little else. Disney-owned *KSFO* in liberal San Francisco is one such station. Some towns have two.

When Edward Monks, a lawyer in Eugene, Oregon, studied the two commercial talk stations in his town, he found "80 hours per week, more than 4,000 hours per year, programmed for Republican and conservative talk shows, without a single second programmed for a Democratic or liberal perspective." Observing that Eugene (a generally progressive town) was "fairly representative," Monks concluded: "Political opinions expressed on talk radio are approaching the level of uniformity that would normally be achieved only in a totalitarian society. There is nothing fair, balanced or democratic about it."

Bringing Back Fairness?

For citizens who value media democracy and the public interest, broadcast regulation of our publicly owned airwaves has reached a low-water mark. In his new book, *Crimes Against Nature*, Robert F. Kennedy Jr. probes the failure of broadcasters to cover the environment, writing, "The FCC's pro-industry, anti-regulatory philosophy has effectively ended the right of access to broadcast television by any but the moneyed interests."

According to *TV Week* [November 2004], a coalition of broadcast giants is currently pondering a legal assault on the Supreme Court's *Red Lion* decision. "Media General and a coalition of major TV network owners—NBC Universal, News Corp. and Viacom—made clear that they are seriously considering an attack on *Red Lion* as part of an industry challenge to an appellate court decision scrapping FCC media ownership deregulation earlier this year."

Considering the many looming problems facing media democracy advocates, *Extra!* asked MAP's Schwartzman why activists should still be concerned about the Fairness Doctrine.

> What has not changed since 1987 is that over-the-air broadcasting remains the most powerful force affecting public opinion, especially on local issues; as public trustees, broadcasters ought to be insuring that they inform the public, not inflame them. That's why we need a Fairness Doctrine. It's not a universal solution. It's not a substitute for reform or for diversity of ownership. It's simply a mechanism to address the most extreme kinds of broadcast abuse.

> *"Any examination . . . will reveal that liberal voices are very well represented on the airwaves."*

Broadcasters Should Not Be Required to Air a Variety of Opposing Views

Brian Fitzpatrick

Effective from 1949 to 1987, the Fairness Doctrine required broadcasters to give airtime to opposing views on current issues. In the following viewpoint, Brian Fitzpatrick states that liberals' arguments to resurrect the law are based on myths about the media. First, the author claims the vast number of news outlets available today defeats the argument that such sources are scarce. Second, although conservatives dominate talk radio, Fitzpatrick alleges that liberals reach a far greater audience across other mediums. Finally, he insists that the historical record shows that the Fairness Doctrine undermined rather than protected free speech. Fitzpatrick is senior editor at the Culture and Media Institute, a division of the conservative media watchdog group Media Research Center.

Brian Fitzpatrick, "Unmasking the Myths Behind the Fairness Doctrine," *Media Research Center*, June 10, 2008. Copyright © 2008 Media Research Center. Reproduced by permission.

As you read, consider the following questions:

1. What broadcast and cable television news sources are available, as stated by Fitzpatrick?

2. How does the author counter the claim that liberals do not have a presence on talk radio?

3. According to the author, how could the Fairness Doctrine have been used against conservatives as a "weapon" in 2008?

The mood was sour on Capitol Hill in June 2007. Powerful members of the Senate were humiliated when they were forced to withdraw a wildly unpopular immigration bill that would have provided de facto amnesty to illegal aliens.

Sen. Dianne Feinstein (D-Calif.) quickly blamed conservative talk radio hosts for the embarrassing defeat. On CNN's *Lou Dobbs Tonight,* Feinstein said, "I listened to talk show hosts drumming up the opposition by using this word 'amnesty' over and over and over again and essentially raising the roil of Americans to the extent that in my 15 years I've never received more hate, or more racist phone calls and threats." . . .

Freedom of speech may be a central pillar upholding American culture, but that didn't prevent recently retired U.S. Sen. Trent Lott (R-Miss.), then a member of the Senate Republican leadership, from casting down the gauntlet: "Talk radio is running America, and we have to deal with that problem."

So how could the Senate deal with those troublesome talkers? A group of senators started speaking publicly about reviving the so-called Fairness Doctrine, an FCC [Federal Communications Commission] regulation suspended by the [Ronald] Reagan administration in 1987. The Fairness Doctrine, first established in 1949, required broadcasters who expressed opinions about controversial issues to give air time to the other side. While its stated intent was to provide balance and increase the amount of opinion available to the public, in practice the Fairness Doctrine stifled free speech by intimidating broadcasters and driving up the cost of broadcasting editorials, and it served as a handy weapon against political opponents. . . .

Efforts to reinstitute the Fairness Doctrine have historically been founded on three arguments: [the scarcity argument, the censorship argument, and the public interest argument]. . . .

Are these arguments valid, or are they myths? We will test the scarcity argument by determining how many news sources are available to Americans, and identifying where Americans turn for their news. We will test the censorship argument by determining the availability of liberal-leaning and conservative-leaning talk show hosts and talk radio stations. We'll also place the argument about talk radio in the context of the media as a whole, by revealing the audience reach of the principal liberal-leaning and conservative-leaning sources in the five major news media: radio, broadcast television, cable television, newspapers and news magazines. While no single talker, radio station, newspaper or broadcast network is 100 percent liberal or conservative, almost every source leans distinctly in one direction or the other. Finally, we will test the public interest argument by reviewing the history of the Fairness Doctrine in practice.

Myth 1: The Scarcity Argument

Does conservative talk radio really dominate the political landscape? That could be true only if talk radio is the prevailing source of news and information in the United States, a doubtful proposition on its face. Given that the liberal party took control of Congress and many state governments in 2006, the notion that conservative talk show hosts are calling the shots in the United States seems dubious.

The original justification for the Fairness Doctrine, which became public policy in 1949, was the "scarcity" argument. The idea was that the airwaves are public property, and the number of wavelengths available on the public airwaves was limited, so the number of radio stations was also limited. Therefore, the government was obligated to make sure broadcasters provided the public with both sides of controversial issues.

Were Americans really deprived of information in 1949? Given that 2,881 radio stations and 98 television stations existed at the time, this argument was questionable from the beginning.

In 2008, the number of news sources has increased exponentially. Americans can choose from at least five major forms of news media: radio, broadcast television, cable television, newspapers and news magazines. These sources are multiplied by the gigantic new factor, the Internet, which makes newspapers, magazines and broadcasting stations, wherever they are located, available to every American with a modem. The World Wide Web itself is home to a tremendous variety of news sources of every political stripe, including news sites, opinion sites, political blogs, news portals, and political activist sites. Alexa, the self-described "Web Information Company," lists 8,693 news sites as of May, 21, 2008, including 3,723 newspaper Web sites. In addition, Alexa lists 3,829 "politics" Web sites. . . .

Still, the biggest news players on the Internet are the traditional news providers. According to several sources, the Internet's most popular news destinations are the Web sites of newspapers, television stations, and radio stations, or portals that lead to the sites of these news organizations. Therefore, we will focus on television, radio, newspapers, and news magazines, rather than Internet political sites and blogs.

Americans can choose from thousands of news sources available around the clock. While the Fairness Doctrine did not apply to non-broadcast media listed here, and presumably would not in the future, our purpose is to establish that an unprecedented number of news and opinion sources are available to the public.

1. *Broadcast Television*. Broadcast television offers seven national news shows per weekday, plus local news shows. The three major commercial networks, ABC, CBS and NBC, each broadcast morning and evening news shows, and PBS airs an evening news show. ABC, NBC, CBS and Fox also have affiliated stations throughout the nation broadcasting one or more local evening news shows. Not even counting TV news magazines and overnight and weekend shows, the typical American can choose from 12 to 15 broadcast television news shows every day.

2. *Cable Television*. Cable television offers 10 national news and public affairs channels available all day long. The typical American cable subscriber can choose from four major cable news and opinion networks, Fox News, CNN, CNN Headline News and MSNBC, which provide virtually continuous news and opinion programming. CNBC, Fox Business Network and Bloomberg offer business news. In addition, C-SPAN broadcasts three channels with separate schedules of live or recorded news events.

3. *Newspapers and News Magazines*. 1,437 daily newspapers were published in America in 2006. Three major weekly news magazines are available throughout the nation.

Newspaper circulation has been dropping for years, but the newspaper remains a vital source of news in America. Many people who once subscribed to newspapers now read them online. According to the Newspaper Association of America, 57 percent of American adults, or 124 million people, read a newspaper on any given day.

4. *Radio*. Americans can choose from 10,000 commercial radio stations and 2,500 noncommercial stations, according to Music Biz Academy. Inside Radio reports that 2,026 of these

stations run a news/talk format, including 1,366 commercial stations and 660 noncommercial stations.

Internet radio broadcasting has made more than 1,000 talk radio stations available. Web Radio lists 991 U.S. news/talk stations available on the Internet, along with 54 international stations. According to Arbitron, 21 percent of the public over the age of 12–52 million people—have listened to radio on the Internet in the past month, and 12 percent–30 million—in the past week.

According to the National Cultural Values Survey conducted for CMI [Culture and Media Institute] in December 2006, most Americans say they rely on either cable or broadcast television as their principal source of news and information. Talk radio, while popular, is not a *principal* source of news. . . .

Myth 2: The Censorship Argument

Are Americans being deprived of access to liberal points of view? Any examination of the talk radio universe will reveal that liberal voices are very well represented on the airwaves. Moreover, talk radio is only one slice of the media pie. Within the "elite media", the major television and cable networks, the leading news magazines, the most circulated newspapers, and most popular news/talk radio programming, liberal news and opinion sources reach a far greater audience than conservative sources.

Have Liberals Been Squeezed Out of Talk Radio?

One linchpin in the effort to restore the Fairness Doctrine is the June 2007 joint report by the Center for American Progress [CAP] and the Free Press, *The Structural Imbalance of Political Talk Radio*. The CAP report analyzes "political talk radio programming on the 257 news/talk stations owned by the five largest commercial station owners," and concludes that 91 percent of their programming is conservative, and nine percent "progressive." In an additional analysis of all news/talk stations in the top 10 markets, the CAP report finds that 76 percent of the programming is conservative and 24 percent is progressive.

The CAP report suffers from a number of structural flaws of its own. For example, its principal study reviews only the five biggest radio station owners, who together own only 18.8 percent of the 1,366 commercial news/talk stations counted by Inside Radio. Also, the report overlooks Air America, a 55-station commercial network created deliberately to spread liberal ideas, and at least 800 noncommercial public radio stations that broadcast liberal news/talk programming.

The CAP report fails completely to document any effort by radio broadcasting companies to "squeeze out" liberal opinion. Readers of the CAP report will search in vain for a single example of a broadcaster canceling a liberal talk show or shutting down a liberal station on ideological grounds.

If liberals were being squeezed out of talk radio, then liberal talkers should be difficult to find on the radio dial, especially in the AM commercial wavelengths. The evidence says otherwise.

1. *Commercial Talk: Anybody who wants to hear liberal talk radio can find it on the airwaves or over the Internet.*

Without a doubt, commercial talk radio is dominated by conservatives, but commercial talk is not an exclusively conservative domain. According to *Talkers Magazine's* March 2008 list of the top commercial issues-oriented talk radio shows, 19 of the nation's top 25 shows are hosted by conservatives or libertarians and 6 are hosted by liberals.

Air America's Ed Schultz, America's most popular liberal talker, appears on more than 100 talk stations, including stations in nine of the top 10 markets, according to his Web site. In addition to broadcasting over the airwaves, 26 of Air America's 55 stations stream over the Internet, making commercial liberal talk radio available 24/7 to anybody with a modem. . . .

2. *Noncommercial Talk: Liberal programming is available throughout the nation on the "public" airwaves.*

The CAP report's greatest flaw is ignoring noncommercial talk radio. Public radio offers consistently liberal news/talk programming produced by four separate networks. The biggest single player in noncommercial issues-oriented radio broadcasting is the government-supported National Public Radio [NPR] network.

The Center for Media Research describes National Public Radio as "an oft unreported, but formidable airwaves presence," the "fourth most listened to radio format," with "an adult audience 75 percent as large as News/Talk, the largest format in the nation." NPR's network provides news and talk programming to at least 860 stations. . . .

Audiences Reached by Major Liberal and Conservative Media.

While the biggest voices in radio lean conservative, liberal-leaning news sources in broadcast television, cable television, newspapers and news magazines reach far more people than conservative-leaning sources.

1. *Broadcast Television News Audience Reach in 2006*
   Liberal-leaning sources: 42.1 million/day
   Conservative-leaning sources: 0

The biggest news medium in the United States is broadcast television, and every major broadcasting network leans to the left. In 2006, ABC, NBC and CBS news programs reached 26.1 million people every evening. The network morning news shows collectively reached 13.6 million per day, and the liberal-leaning PBS evening news show reached a daily audience of 2.4 million.

No major conservative-leaning broadcast television network exists, so conservative-leaning broadcast audience reach is 0. . . .

2. *Cable Television News Audience Reach in 2006*
   Liberal-leaning sources: 182.8 million/month
   Conservative-leaning sources: 61.6 million/month

"Wait a minute!" you cry. Am I really saying the three liberal-leaning cable news networks, CNN, CNN Headline News and MSNBC, together draw three times as many people as the single conservative-leaning network, Fox News Channel? Doesn't Fox have nine of the 10 highest rated shows?

The answers are Yes and Yes. Cable TV ratings are based on the average number of viewers watching at any given moment during the daytime or evening. Fox News Channel viewers tend to stay with Fox shows for longer periods of time, while the liberal networks' viewers are more likely to watch for just a few minutes at a time, so Fox programs have more eyes glued to the screen at any given moment and Fox shows generate higher ratings. Far more sets of eyes, however, visit the liberal cable networks.

Cable ratings are not unimportant, but measuring average audience at any given moment doesn't tell us what we want to know. Because we're assessing the audience reach of liberal and conservative news sources, we're more interested in the total number of viewers who watch each network.

Cable TV measures total audience on a monthly basis— and the monthly "cumes" tell a different story from the averages. As a group, the liberal-leaning cable networks reach about three times more viewers per month than conservative-leaning Fox News.

3. *Top 25 Newspapers by Circulation in 2006*

    Liberal-leaning newspapers: 11.7 million/day

    Conservative-leaning papers: 1.3 million/day

    Mixed liberal/conservative paper: 2.1 million/day

America's leading newspapers overwhelmingly tilt to the left. Twenty-one of the 25 newspapers with the highest daily circulation lean liberal, three lean conservative, and one paper fits in neither category. The paper with the second greatest circulation, *The Wall Street Journal*, has a famously conservative editorial page, but the *Journal's* news pages are among the nation's most liberal, so we list the *WSJ* as "mixed." . . .

4. *Talk Radio Audience Reach in 2007 (estimates)*

Liberal-leaning source: 24.5 million/week

Conservative-leaning: 87 million/week

No solid, publicly available numbers exist for talk radio audience reach. Only *Talkers Magazine* compiles a list of the top commercial talk shows by size of audience, and many people in the radio industry passionately dispute *Talkers'* numbers and rankings.

For example, *Talkers* estimates Rush Limbaugh's audience at 14 million per week, while the corporation behind Limbaugh's show, Premiere Radio Networks, asserts that Limbaugh reaches 20 million. Some hosts told CMI they accept their *Talkers* estimate, and others say they're undercounted. One company actually said one of its shows is overcounted. For the sake of argument we will use *Talkers'* data, which fall somewhere in the middle of the range of estimated audience figures.

No complete picture of talk radio's audience reach can ignore the noncommercial side of the equation—public radio. According to the Project for Excellence in Journalism (PEJ), the news/talk shows of the four major public radio networks collectively reach 14 million people per week, an audience that rivals the biggest commercial talk shows. The noncommercial public radio networks, unfortunately, do not provide comprehensive audience reach statistics for their shows. Therefore, we are considering public radio as a whole alongside our list of the top 25 talk show hosts. Even factoring in public radio, conservative dominance of news/talk radio is clear: the leading conservative and libertarian-leaning sources reach about 3.6 times more people per week than the leading liberal-leaning sources. . . .

5. *Weekly News Magazine Circulation in 2007*

Liberal-leaning sources: 8.5 million/week

Conservative-leaning: 0

The weekly news magazine medium is dominated by the Big Three: *Time, Newsweek* and *U.S. News and World Report.* Like the biggest medium, broadcast television, the news world's smallest major medium is composed exclusively of liberal-leaning sources. . . .

Myth 3: The Public Interest Argument

At first blush the Fairness Doctrine seems very sensible, even obvious. Who wouldn't want broadcasters to provide both sides of controversial issues? Wouldn't the public benefit from hearing even more opinions?

The historical record, however, belies the assertion that the so-called Fairness Doctrine facilitates more speech. Broadcasters, intimidated by the potential difficulties and expense of providing alternative views whenever they aired a controversial opinion, often chose simply to avoid controversial topics altogether. The Project for Excellence in Journalism, in its report *The State of the News Media 2007*, asserts that the result of the Fairness Doctrine "was that radio talk programs consisted primarily of general (non-political) talk and advice. The big names were people like Michael Jackson in Los Angeles, whose program included interviews with celebrities, authors, and civic leaders." PEJ observes that "the modern era in talk radio effectively began with the Federal Communications Commission's repeal of the Fairness Doctrine in 1987."

It's no wonder many broadcasters apparently were intimidated by the Fairness Doctrine, given the ugly history of politically inspired infringement on broadcasters' freedom of speech when the Fairness Doctrine was in force. . . .

The Fairness Doctrine has been used repeatedly as a weapon to chill the speech of political opponents. Do the current proponents of the doctrine plan to use it the same way? Statements by the politicians who want to bring it back—for example, Sen. Lott declaring, "Talk radio is running America, and we have to deal with that problem"—strongly suggest that their purpose is to use it again as a weapon. Leading Democrats in the House of Representatives plan to restore the Fairness Doctrine strictly to deny Republicans a perceived advantage in the 2008 election, according to a May 2007 article in *The American Spectator*, "Her Royal Fairness." The *Spectator* quotes a senior adviser to House Speaker Nancy Pelosi:

> "First, [Democrats] failed on the radio airwaves with Air America, no one wanted to listen. Conservative radio is a huge threat and political advantage for Republicans and we have had to find a way to limit it. Second, it looks like the Republicans are going to have someone in the presidential race who has access to media in ways our folks don't want, so we want to make sure the GOP [Grand Old Party] has no advantages going into 2008." . . .

America does not need the so-called Fairness Doctrine.

Americans enjoy overwhelming, unprecedented access to news and opinion from a practically unlimited number of sources representing every conceivable value system and school of thought. While no individual news medium is perfectly balanced in the variety of opinions it provides to the public, the sheer volume of information provided by the news media, increased exponentially by the Internet, guarantees that anybody can find liberal or conservative takes on public policy issues at any time of day or night. We do not need government to dictate to radio broadcasters, or anybody else, that they must counter their own opinions by subsidizing the presentation of opinions they disbelieve.

Periodical Bibliography

The following articles have been selected to supplement the diverse views presented in this chapter.

Dennis AuBuchon "Free Speech and the Fairness Doctrine," *American Chronicle*, March 19, 2009.

Greg Beato "The Spin We Love to Hate: Do We Really Want News Without a Point of View?" *Reason*, December 2008.

Jeffrey Chester "Time for a Digital Fairness Doctrine," *AlterNet*, October 19, 2004.

Edward W. Gillespie "Media Realism: How the GOP Should Handle Increasingly Biased Journalists," *National Review*, April 6, 2009.

Nicole Hemmer "Liberals, Too, Should Reject the Fairness Doctrine," *Christian Science Monitor*, November 25, 2008.

R. Court Kirkwood "What Did or Didn't Happen at Duke," *New American*, September 18, 2006.

Richard Perez-Pena "Online Watchdog Sniffs for Media Bias," *New York Times*, October 15, 2008.

Eugene Robinson "(White) Women We Love," *Washington Post*, June 10, 2005.

Joseph Somsel "Megaphone Envy and the Fairness Doctrine," *American Thinker*, March 19, 2009.

Adam Thierer "The Media Cornucopia," *City Journal*, Spring 2007.

Evan Thomas "The Myth of Objectivity," *Newsweek*, March 10, 2008.

OPPOSING
VIEWPOINTS®
SERIES

CHAPTER 2

Does Media Ownership Need More or Less Regulation?

Chapter Preface

U.S. Secretary of Labor Hilda Solis, in a September 2007 article on reclaimthemedia.org, declares that the "state of minority media ownership in America is in crisis." The main reason, she argues, "[T]he Federal Communications Commission (FCC) under chairman Kevin Martin has simply failed in recent years to address the enormous disparity in minority ownership, including women. Their historic neglect is simply unacceptable and cannot be allowed continue." Solis draws upon statistics provided by the Stop Big Media campaign, a project of the nonprofit media group Free Press. According to the campaign, as of October 2007, ethnic minorities make up about a third of the American population, but the numbers of minorities who own commercial broadcast radio stations are minuscule: Latinos own 2.9 percent, African Americans 3.1 percent, and Asians 1 percent. As for commercial broadcast television stations, Stop Big Media states that minorities own 3.15 percent, and women, who comprise 51 percent of the American population, own 5.87 percent.

Stop Big Media also upholds that the growth of media conglomerates, such as Viacom, News Corporation, and the Walt Disney Company, and mergers not only limit minority and female ownership and representation in the media, but threaten political and social pluralism as whole. Ben Scott, policy director of Free Press, in an October 2008 article by Sascha Meinrath on Govtech.com, contends that the regulation of media ownership "is not a left-right issue—it unites a wide variety of organizations concerned about the impact of concentrated media on the diversity of opinion a democracy requires."

Nonetheless, proponents maintain that relaxing restrictions, such as the FCC's decision in 2001 to allow dual ownership of major television networks, allows media conglomerates to provide a wider range of programs and content. Policy analyst Jason M. Thomas insists in an April 2001 FreedomWorks.com article, "Only Viacom-owned UPN and AOL-Time Warner's WB [now the CW Television Network] cater most of their programming to unique tastes and niche advertisers. UPN boast[ed] two of the most popular shows among African American audiences, *Moesha* and *The Hughleys*, while WB's most successful shows [were] geared specifically for young audiences." In Thomas's view, a consolidated media is a plural media: "Consolidation allows television programmers to appeal to different audiences, and, more importantly, to attract more advertising revenue through different channels. In this way, the profit motive encourages, rather than stifles, diversity."

Clearly, views regarding media ownership, concentration, and regulation are far from a consensus. The authors in the following viewpoints share their opinions of how FCC rules— and changes to them—affect broadcast networks and press organizations nationally, locally, economically, and socially.

| "When the smaller [media] businesses are gone, where will the new ideas come from?"

Media Monopolies Are a Serious Problem

Charlie Cray

Loosened rules on media ownership make it easier for large corporations to dominate local markets, argues Charlie Cray in the following viewpoint. He claims that, in 2003, the Federal Communications Commission (FCC) raised the number of radio stations media conglomerates can own and their share of the national television audience they can reach through ownership of local stations. Consequently, the author claims that not only are diversity and competition in the media less protected, the social costs of corporate consolidation have been wrought at the local and national level. Cray is a policy analyst and director of the Center for Corporate Policy in Washington, DC, and former associate editor of Multinational Monitor.

Charlie Cray, "Dissecting Bush: Bush Administration Policies Under the Microscope," *Multinational Monitor*, May-June 2004. Reproduced by permission.

As you read, consider the following questions:

1. How does Cray compare the roles media executives and their opponents played in the FCC's drafting of the changed ownership rules?

2. As stated by Cray, what happened in North Dakota as a result of Clear Channel's increased ownership of radio stations?

3. According to the author, what groups objected to the FCC's change in ownership rules?

In a move that critics say opens the doors to media conglomerates' domination of local markets, the Federal Communications Commission (FCC) [June 2003] loosened some of the few remaining restrictions on corporate media monopolies.

In the end, the decision may end up looking like a hollow victory for companies like Viacom, CBS, Disney and Rupert Murdoch's News Corporation, since the FCC's decision provoked unprecedented grassroots engagement with the issue and widespread opposition across the political spectrum.

The new rules loosen "cross ownership" standards that restrict media conglomerates from owning newspapers, television stations and radio stations in the same local markets; raise the number of radio stations one company can own in a single market; and raise the share of the national TV audience that any single company through ownership of local stations can reach to 45 percent, an increase from 35 percent (the standard was later reduced to 39 percent by an irate Congress.)

[Former] FCC Commissioner Michael Powell led the drive to loosen the rules on media monopolies. "Monopoly is not illegal by itself in the United States," Powell asserted in early 2002. "There is something healthy about letting innovators try to capture markets."

The Changing Media Landscape

Powell claimed that court decisions required the FCC to strike down existing broadcast-ownership limits promoting diversity, localism and competition. Many of the rules extended back decades. According to Powell, the courts held that the growth of cable TV, satellite broadcasts, the Internet and other technologies had long ago rendered these rules obsolete.

"Keeping the rules exactly as they are, as some so stridently suggest, was not a viable option," Powell explained.

Yet opponents pointed out that the courts did not require the FCC to gut the rules, but simply use up-to-date market facts to explain them.

FCC Commissioner Jonathan Adelstein, who voted against Powell, called the decision "the most sweeping and destructive rollback of consumer-protection rules in the history of American broadcasting."

"This plan is likely to damage the media landscape for generations to come," Adelstein said. "In the end, this order simply makes it easier for existing media giants to gobble up more outlets and fortify their already massive market power."

Adelstein and Commissioner Michael Copps, who also voted against Powell, were not alone in opposition to the rule changes. The FCC received an unprecedented 750,000 public comments on the proposals, over 99.9 percent of them reportedly in opposition.

But Powell dismissed the outpouring of opposition, for failing to address the specific technical questions at issue. The comments "didn't provide the kind of record evidence that leads to very specific decisions," he suggested. But as Common Cause and others who encouraged people to comment point out, the FCC had failed to make any formal, detailed proposal available to the public, Congress, or even Copps and Adelstein until three weeks before the vote.

The Five Conglomerates

Five global-dimension firms, operating with many of the characteristics of a cartel, own most of the newspapers, magazines, book publishers, motion picture studios, and radio and television stations in the United States. Each medium they own, whether magazines or broadcast stations, covers the entire country, and the owners prefer stories and programs that can be used everywhere and anywhere. Their media products reflect this. The programs broadcast in the six empty stations in Minot, N. Dak., were simultaneously being broadcast in New York City.

These five conglomerates are Time Warner, by 2003 the largest media firm in the world; The Walt Disney Company; Murdoch's News Corporation, based in Australia; Viacom; and Bertelsmann, based in Germany. Today, none of the dominant media companies bother with dominance merely in a single medium. Their strategy has been to have major holdings in all the media, from newspapers to movie studios. This gives each of the five corporations and their leaders more communications power than was exercised by any despot or dictatorship in history.

Ben H. Bagdikian, The New Media Monopoly.
Boston, MA: Beacon Press, 2004.

Media Executives Favored

Getting access to the draft rules was apparently not much of a problem for 63 executives from the nation's top broadcast companies—including Rupert Murdoch of NewsCorp and Mel Karmazin [formerly] of Viacom—who reportedly met with FCC staff over 70 times behind closed doors before the commission reached its decision. In fact, the *Wall Street Journal* reported on the day of the vote, Bear Stearns media analyst Victor Miller helped FCC staff draft the regulations themselves.

Meanwhile, the Center for Public Integrity reported on another indicator of close ties between FCC regulators and the media they regulate: FCC staff had accepted more than 2,500 junkets worth nearly $2.8 million from the telecommunications and broadcast industries [from 1996 to 2004].

By contrast, the FCC held just one official public hearing before issuing its new rules and met with opponents to discuss the rules in their offices just five times.

"In the digital age, you don't need a nineteenth-century whistle-stop tour to hear from America," Powell explained.

Concerned about the lack of attention the media itself was paying to the issue, commissioners Copps and Adelstein attended a series of informal public meetings organized by the Center for Digital Democracy and local, nonpartisan civic groups across the country.

The meetings highlighted the impact the new rules would have at the local level, where the media giants would soon be able to own the daily newspaper, two or three TV stations, and up to eight radio stations.

Concentration's Costs

Recent changes in the commercial radio market illustrate the potential threat that the new rules could pose. After Congress removed radio ownership limits in 1996, Clear Channel's list of radio stations grew from just 43 in 1995 to 1,233 stations by 2004.

The impact of the Texas company's monopoly on local culture and even national security is illustrated by what happened after a freight train derailed in Minot, North Dakota in 2002. A deadly cloud of anhydrous ammonia floated over the small city, posing a public emergency. Police called town radio stations to attempt to alert the public. But all of the six radio stations in the city of 36,500 were owned by Clear Channel, which had largely done away with local programming and local staff. Nobody answered the phones for more than an hour and a half. Three hundred people were hospitalized, some partially blinded. Pets and livestock were killed.

The propagandistic power of Clear Channel's monopoly was also clear during the [George W.] Bush administration's buildup to the war in Iraq, when Clear Channel stations organized a series of flag-waving pro-war rallies in Atlanta, Cleveland, San Antonio, Cincinnati and other cities. (Clear Channel vice chair Tom Hicks is an old Texas buddy of [former] President Bush, from whom he bought the Texas Rangers.) Although Clear Channel promoted the rallies on its corporate web site, company officials claim there was no corporate directive that stations organize the rallies, or that the rallies had anything to do with pending regulatory matters the company had before the FCC.

Objections to the FCC ownership rules have come from a diverse army of groups from across the political spectrum, including the National Rifle Association, religious and civil rights groups, consumer, labor and even certain industry groups, such as the National Association of Broadcasters, which represents smaller broadcasting corporations.

Media moguls Barry Diller and CNN founder Ted Turner also spoke up against the rules.

"When the smaller businesses are gone, where will the new ideas come from?" Turner asked. "Under the new rules, there will be more consolidation, and more news sharing. That means laying off reporters or, in other words, downsizing the workforce that helps us see our problems and makes us think about solutions. Even more troubling are the warning signs that large media corporations—with massive market power— could abuse that power by slanting news coverage in ways that serve their political or financial interests."

Yet Powell and the other commissioners wouldn't budge. But after the FCC's 3-2 decision, the battle was far from over. In some ways, it had just begun: A bipartisan group of senators led by Byron Dorgan, D-North Dakota, and Trent Lott, R-Mississippi, responded by leading an effort to overturn the rule changes. They won a 55-40 vote to overturn the rules in the Senate.

With over 200 members of the House of Representatives demanding that the matter be brought to a vote, Republican leaders struggled to keep a lid on the issue. To avoid a situation where Bush might have to veto a popular law in an election year, Republican leaders instead forced the matter into an omnibus budget bill towards the end of 2003, where they managed to rig a "compromise" that left the big conglomerates happy. The omnibus bill kept the Powell rules in place, but capped TV station ownership at 39 percent—just high enough to keep Viacom and Murdoch's News Corporation in compliance with the law.

The battle was also taken to the courts. The Media Access Project filed a petition on behalf of the Philadelphia-based Prometheus Radio Project with the Third Circuit Court of Appeals, arguing that the rule changes violated federal law. The court agreed to hear the case and issued an immediate stay so that the rule changes would not be put into effect until the case was decided.

Meanwhile, in November [2004] more than 2,000 activists converged in Madison, Wisconsin for a landmark national conference on media reform, a sign that the battle against corporate control of the media was escalating.

As Michael Copps said in explaining his dissenting vote against the FCC's decision, "The obscurity of this issue that many have relied upon in the past, where only a few dozen inside-the-beltway lobbyists understood this issue, is gone forever."

| "'Mass media' after all, means that it
| caters to a mass interest."

Media Monopolies Are a Myth

Ben Compaine

In the following viewpoint excerpted from his testimony given to the U.S. Senate's Committee on Commerce, Science, and Transportation, Ben Compaine argues that rather than being consolidated and under vast corporate control, the media is now more diverse and accessible than in previous decades. First, Compaine upholds that major networks' viewer market share has significantly declined. Also, he states that the radio market is only concentrated in comparison to others and not shaped by a few influential sellers. Finally, Compaine insists that the Internet has become a medium unprecedented in its expansion of consumer choice, distribution of content, and competition. Compaine teaches technology entrepreneurship at Northeastern University in Boston, and he co-wrote Who Owns the Media? Competition and Concentration in the Mass Media Industry.

Ben Compaine, "Testimony of Ben Compaine, United States Senate, Committee on Commerce, Science and Transportation," compaine.bcompany.com, September 28, 2004. Reproduced by permission.

As you read, consider the following questions:

1. How does Compaine support his assertion that major networks reach fewer households now than they did in the 1970s?

2. How does the author characterize National Public Radio?

3. As stated by Compaine, why is Congress unable to effectively "micromanage" television and radio regulation?

M y name is Ben Compaine. I've been tracking media ownership trends since the first edition of my book, *Who Owns the Media?*, was compiled in 1978. Let me note up front that I have never been employed by any major media company nor have I been a paid consultant for any major media company.

The concerns you address today about media ownership are not new ones. In 1978 the Federal Trade Commission [FTC] held two days of public hearings in this city as part of its investigation of mergers and acquisitions in publishing. After sifting through the anecdotal stories of the critics and the pessimistic scenarios of doomsayers, the FTC under President [Jimmy] Carter could find no basis for any rule making, policy changes or legislative suggestions.

But the focus in 2004 is on television and radio—areas which have a richer history and basis of government regulation and court involvement. So this morning I will restrict my comments to these areas.

I start by questioning one of the fundamental assumptions of media ownership: that it is more concentrated than ever. Typical is a *Seattle Times* editorial that stated flatly, "The news industry in America is already far down the road to media concentration." In the same editorial they cite CNN, Fox News,

National Public Radio—all separately owned sources of news that have been added to the media menu in the last two decades. None have been subtracted.

The viewpoint I take is measuring whether consumers of the media—all of us—have access to a greater universe of diverse content from more sources than 15 or 20 years ago. Or is there a concentration resulting in fewer sources and implicitly less diversity? This applies to entertainment, culture, news and opinion. I suspect we would all agree that a goal is to assure enough players to ensure that sources and diversity are sufficient to satisfy small as well as mass audiences.

I want to make three points today:

First, that television is more competitive than it has ever been, in number of different networks and owners of networks. The audience is more fragmented than it has ever been. Far from being more concentrated, by important measures it is far less so.

Second, that radio is more concentrated only in comparison to an extremely fragmented industry that existed before 1996. No other industry could have expanded 10 fold and still have no owner hold more properties at the end than at the start of that period. In absolute terms radio is still highly competitive and as diverse as ever.

Third, that the Internet is already proving itself as a popular, ubiquitous and effective medium for expanding distribution of both video and audio for more players and access to more sources of information for consumers than we could have reasonably expected even 15 years ago. And the technology continues to improve to provide more competition for existing players.

I will elaborate briefly on each point. More comprehensive data on these and additional points are in a paper that I just completed that will be made available by the New Millennium Research Council here in Washington within a few weeks. I urge you to look through that paper.

Information Cannot Be Monopolized

The most frequent justification offered for restricting media ownership is to prevent monopolization of viewpoints expressed in the media, i.e., to protect diversity in ideas. But the media are merely conduits for information of every sort, and information cannot be monopolized where the government does not practice censorship. The media are an implementation of free speech, not its enemy. Although this article is not the venue for a treatise on the follies of antitrust law over the past century (that has of late found potential monopolies in pickles, intense mints, and premium ice cream), let it at least be offered for consideration that there is no such phenomenon as a media monopoly unanswerable to the rest of society, and to the economy potentially arrayed against the media, if it were to abuse its station in society.

Clyde Wayne Crews Jr.,
"A Defense of Media Monopoly,"
Communications Lawyer, *vol. 23, no. 3,*
Winter 2003–2004.

Television

The viewer market share of the three traditional television networks—CBS, ABC, NBC—has declined substantially since 1980. During the 1960s and 1970s, on a typical weekday evening, the three networks on average were watched by about 56% of all households with televisions. In 2003 on a weekday evening during prime time those networks had only a 20% rating. Adding in the audiences they and their parent companies have gained through networks available by multichannel means such as cable or satellite, in 2003 their combined audience was *less than* in the 1970s and into the 1980s.

Let me make that as clear as possible. *In 2003, Viacom, with CBS plus all its cable networks, Disney, with ABC and its cable networks, and NBC, with its newly acquired cable networks, accounted for 18% fewer households during prime time than in the pre-merger, pre-cable three network days.*

Moreover, there is additional competition from newer networks, including Time Warner's WB [now the CW Television Network] and News Corporation's Fox. The five broadcast networks together aggregated to a 26% rating. Adding in the rating of these five broadcast networks with the cable networks owned by the same corporate family (e.g., CNN, HBO, etc. with WB), the five major providers of television programming accounted for an average 51% rating in December 2003. This was less than three broadcast networks had into the 1980s.

In television we all know that there are orders of magnitude more choices today than 25 years ago and, even with numerous acquisitions and startups by the old networks and their new parents, we have more networks, from more owners than in the days of three networks and seven station limits for any owner.

Radio

On to radio. Issues need a context. Taken out of context, the radio industry has seen substantial consolidation in the last decade. The largest operator of radio stations in 2004 owned about 8.6% of the almost 14,000 radio stations nationwide. The four largest groups owned under 15% of all stations, a total not even close to any level of oligopoly by antitrust standards.

The context, however, is that of an industry that had more than tripled in the number of stations over three decades with no change in the limits of station ownership. In 1947, when a *de facto* limit of 13 stations to an owner was in place, there were about 1200 radio stations. By 1980 the limit was the same, but there were over 8700 stations. A single owner could hold no more than 0.16% of stations nationally. In 1990, by which time the cap had been raised to 12 stations, we were closing in on 11,000 stations.

So it should be no surprise that, like a bottle of seltzer that had been well shook, when the cap was removed in 1996 the industry burst into [a] long delayed hive of activity. Even if the ownership limits had been eased from 1947 into the 1990s to maintain the same ratio of ownership to the number of stations, the cap would have been about 88 and the changes we have seen in recent years would have looked far less dramatic.

Often lost in the radio discussion is that National Public Radio, a loose network of more than 700 not-for-profit radio stations that broadcast common national programming for much of the day, would be the second largest radio chain. It claims to be available everywhere in the U.S. There is also the growing interest in the national satellite-distributed radio services. In January [2004] they had 1.6 million subscribers. At their current rate of growth that is expect to reach 4 million by the end of [that] year.

To be sure, the number of separate owners of radio stations in local markets is lower than prior to the lessening of regulatory limits in the 1990s. Still, larger markets have 15 or more separate owners—in addition to noncommercial stations—and in most of even the smallest markets there are more competitors in radio than television and newspapers combined.

Finally, as a segue to my comments on the role of the Internet, thousands of radio and radio-like stations are available via the Internet. Stations are available from around the globe. Many of those with the highest listenership were owned by non-broadcasters. About 40% of listeners accessed stations from outside their local market.

Internet

Barely 10 years after its "coming out" as a consumer medium, about two-thirds of Americans are using the Internet for everything from e-mail to news to weather to government forms to shopping, porn, sharing family photos, listening to radio and watching "television." The Internet already has profound implications for access to information.

Of the five largest media companies, the Web sites of only one (Time Warner) are among the top 10 organizations whose Web sites get the most unique visitors per month. The sites run by federal government agencies are among the most frequented.

In 2004 for the first time more Internet households had broadband than used dial-up connections. With research that shows that households with always-on broadband used the Internet more than narrowband users, the expectation is that Internet access for information, commerce and communications will continue to grow.

The number of hours spent listening to Internet radio grew by triple digits between 2003 and the same period in 2004. Users with broadband spend far more time using Internet radio than dial-up users.

In addition, new devices are becoming available to make Internet radio accessible apart from a personal computer, including access via various wireless technologies. Indeed, video and film via the Internet are on the verge of becoming more mainstream. As some of the local telephone carriers upgrade their systems with fiber optic cable to the curb or the home, the transmission speed of downloads will be competitive with cable and satellite services. Devices are on the market that allow even today's broadband users to download movies and video programming for storage on personal video recorders for viewing at their convenience.

Need to Consider Choices Available, Not Choices Made

[In 2003] this committee heard testimony from my friend [author, professor and director of Columbia University's Institute for Tele-Information] Eli Noam. He has completed some landmark work on the revenue side of the media industry. It is helpful, yet only part of the mosaic that is media competition. A substantial piece of the debate must be on sources of content and distribution avenues that are readily and inexpensively available to most consumers. We need to look beyond what percent of the audience watches what company's shows at any given time. A more important measure is whether viewers and listeners can, should they choose to do so, just as easily watch or listen to content from a reasonable number of other sources. "Mass media" after all, means that it caters to a mass interest. It is unlikely that there should be 20 television shows on at the same time that are all mass interest.

As television viewers, most of us at any given moment are in the 75% that is watching one of [the] programs that derive from a small number of providers. But at other times, we are part of the other 25% that is divided into many small audiences watching one of the many other providers. Both the 75% and the 25% are not the same people all the time.

Policy Issues

My findings lead me [to] an observation and a question for policy-makers:

- The observation is that while Congress certainly has the prerogative, it cannot micromanage effectively television and radio regulation. The technology and industry are changing too fast for the way Congress does and should work. I believe the current FCC [Federal Communications Commission] understands the forces and trends well and should be given latitude, to do its job.

Though a cumbersome process—as is most of democracy—the courts have served as a viable check on as well as motivator to the Commission.

- My question may be more controversial. When almost 90% of households view television via a cable or satellite connection, why are we still making a regulatory distinction between broadcast and other avenues of video distribution? There is a certain paradox in CBS being fined for the Janet Jackson Super Bowl fiasco [during the 2004 half time show, Jackson's breast was exposed briefly] when more than 90% of those viewing were doing so over cable or satellite. If ESPN had carried the same thing there would have been no fine (though perhaps the same controversy). The value of a television broadcast license today is almost exclusively in the "must carry" mandate that goes with it. If that were retained should broadcasters be allowed to turn off their transmitters, my hunch is that the FCC would be flooded with returned spectrum as licensees would opt to jettison what little is left of their public service obligation and regulation and move their operation directly to a multichannel platform.

Thank you for having me here. I expect I've raised as many questions as I've answered and would be delighted to respond to any you have, now or later.

> "The very reason that merging newspa-
> pers and broadcast outlets under one
> owner makes economic sense ... often
> fails to serve the public interest."

The Newspaper-broadcast Cross-ownership Ban Should Be Preserved

Common Cause

In December 2007, the Federal Communications Commission (FCC) loosened its restrictions of cross-ownership, allowing companies to own a major newspaper and television or radio station in the same market. In the following viewpoint, Common Cause contends that without these restrictions, the incentives of corporations will outweigh public interest. According to Common Cause, a cross-owned media will lead to selective coverage of the media business, marginalization of critical and diverse voices, and organizational promotion in the place of journalism. Furthermore, the group alleges that in cross-owned companies, editorial values, integrity, and staff will suffer for business and economic reasons. Founded in 1970, the Washington, DC-based Common Cause is a non-partisan citizen's lobbying group.

As you read, consider the following questions:

1. In Common Cause's view, how did the *Atlanta Journal-Constitution* ignore diverse voices?

2. According to the group, how did the *Arizona Republic* compromise journalistic integrity for organizational promotion?

3. How did cross-ownership hurt the *Hartford Courant*, as described by Common Cause?

For more than 30 years, the Federal Communications Commission has had a rule in place that prevents one company from owning both the local newspaper and the local TV station in one community. The reasons behind the ban on newspaper-broadcast cross-ownership are clear: A single owner deprives a community of important diverse sources of news, information and opinion.

As journalism professor Douglas Gomery wrote in 2002, there are even better reasons to keep the newspaper-broadcaster cross-ownership ban in place today than there were in 1975. A handful of media giants now owns most of the major sources of our information: newspapers, television stations, radio stations, and cable systems. The media behemoths are more concerned about pleasing shareholders and increasing profits than serving their respective communities. The number of layoffs at the New York Times Co. and Tribune Company attests to the power of Wall Street, not Main Street, to dictate the resources that are available to cover news, particularly local news.

The very reason that merging newspapers and broadcast outlets under one owner makes economic sense—the ability to maximize the productivity of news staffs by sharing resources, reducing competition, and cutting costs—often fails to serve the public interest when it reduces the amount of independently produced news and information available in a local community.

A cross-owned media offers the following dangers:

- Giving the community inadequate coverage of the media business itself

- Ignoring diverse voices, particularly critics

- Avoiding enterprise reporting

- Confusing promotion with substantive journalism

- Choosing synergy over a quality product

- Compromising editorial values for business reasons

- Sharing resources and staff in ways that dilute, rather than enhance the quality of the cross-owned news staffs

Media that are not cross-owned can be guilty of the same sins, but in media markets with diverse owners, those sins are more likely to come to light, and less likely to harm viewers, readers and listeners, who have other sources of news and information about local events and issues. . . .

Going Easy on a Media Outlet That Shares a Common Owner: The Tampa Story

If newspapers and TV stations share the same parent in one market, it is likely that each media outlet will go easy when the other media property is criticized.

Consider, for example, what happened when NBC affiliate WFLA-TV was excoriated by journalists across the country for its practice of charging guests on its morning magazine show, *Daytime*, $2,500 for a four-to-six-minute segment with the program's hosts.

Washington Post media columnist Howard Kurtz wrote three stories about the incident. His first story was published on Oct. 16, 2003, and was headlined, "Florida TV Station

Cashes in on Interview 'Guests.'" Kurtz ultimately returned to the subject three times, and the *Post* also published an editorial calling the practice of posing advertising content as stories on the magazine format show as a "descent to pay-for-play journalism."

But the *Tampa Tribune*, which shares the same parent, Media General Corp., with WFLA, took a kinder, gentler approach in its story, which was published on Oct. 18, two days after Kurtz aimed his first critical salvo.

The *Tribune's* 590-word story, which ran on page two of its metro section, describes *Daytime* as an "advertiser-driven talk show," and quotes only WFLA executives who countered Kurtz's criticism by asserting that *Daytime* was not a news show. "[H]e (Kurtz) inaccurately characterized *Daytime* as being journalism," WFLA's president and general manager [Eric Land] told the *Tribune*. "*Daytime* is an entertainment program with no journalism elements," Land added.

The *Tribune's* coverage so riled Elizabeth Rose, a former public affairs officer for the Federal Communications Commission (FCC), that she penned an op-ed for *Broadcasting and Cable*, in which she charged that the "co-owned newspaper did not break this legitimate media story unfolding right in its own building. When the paper did get around to reporting it, its version read like a corporate press release. This is a case study of why TV/newspaper cross-ownership is bad for democracy," Rose concluded.

It was only after Senator John McCain (R-AZ) asked the FCC to examine the practice of selling airtime to advertisers that the *Tribune* gave any substantive coverage of the scandal at WFLA.

Shutting Out Diverse Voices: The Atlanta Story

On March 25, 2002, a contingent of African-American civic and religious leaders staged a protest rally outside the entrance of the *Atlanta Journal-Constitution* to complain about the newspaper's coverage of the city's African-American political leaders. The protestors included the head of the Atlanta Economic Development Corporation, the president of 100 Black Men of America, and The Concerned Black Clergy.

But the *Journal* did not cover the protest demonstration. Neither did WSB-TV, although, according to African-American newsweekly, the *Atlanta Inquirer*, a WSB-TV cameraman taped the entire event. Both the *Journal-Constitution*, Atlanta's only daily newspaper, and WSB-TV, the ratings leader for local news, are owned by Cox Enterprises. Cox also owns WSB-AM, its leading news/talk radio station.

Atlanta's major media also ignored another major story in its own backyard. When Federal Communications Commissioners Michael Copps and Jonathan Adelstein held a hearing in Atlanta, on the FCC's proposed media consolidation rules in May 2003, Salon.com covered the event, which drew 600 people.

But neither the *Atlanta Journal-Constitution* nor WSB radio or television alerted its readers or listeners that a meeting was going to be held, nor did a story on the event, according to *Salon*. The only way the crowd found out about it was by reading the city's alternative weekly, or tuning in to two community radio stations, WRFG or WRAS.

Confusing Promotion with Substantive Journalism: The Phoenix Story

Sometimes when a newspaper and a television station join forces on a community news/public service project, the reporting does not go deep enough. That seems to have been the case in Phoenix, Arizona, where Gannett owns the state's largest newspaper, the *Arizona Republic*, and television outlet, KPNX-TV. The co-owned media outlets teamed up to push a special effort on swimming pool safety.

The newspaper's promotion and the TV station's outreach both took the same approach: warning parents to watch their children around pools, particularly during the summer months. On Labor Day in 2002, the *Republic* pronounced victory, and declared a 50 percent drop in drowning deaths.

But a thoughtful investigative story, the result of one year of research, by the alternative weekly in town, the *Phoenix New Times*, offered a different point of view. The *New Times* contended that the safety campaign's results were more tenuous, and that drownings did not end with the formal end of the summer season. Indeed, the total number of childhood drownings in Phoenix in 2002 was down by 3, from 15 to 12, a 20 percent decline. Further, a careful read of the statistics and historical record seemed to indicate that drownings were clustered in a number of neighborhoods in decline in West Phoenix, and that the lack of a proper fence around pools, rather than inadequate parental supervision during pool time, was a major cause of the deaths and near-deaths from drowning.

Ironically, the same story extolling the promotion effort buried a much more troubling fact: Efforts by Phoenix firefighters to supply disadvantaged Phoenix families with free pool fences had fallen far short of their goal. Of the 500 requests for pool fences the firefighters received, they were able to help only one in 20 families. The firefighters resorted to a lottery to choose the winners. In a more competitive market, one of these leading news outlets may have seized on this disturbing fact.

Two years later, the *Republic* came to understand the importance of pool fences. While still championing the success of efforts by the newspaper and its co-owned TV news operation, 12 News, for its pool public awareness programs, the *Republic* cited statistics from the Arizona Child Fatality Review Team that found that from 1995 to 1999, "only four of 81 drowning deaths by children younger than 5 occurred in backyard pools that had an adequate pool fence and a properly functioning, locked gate."

Substituting Synergy for a Better Product: The Hartford Story

Meteorologist Dr. Mel Goldstein had all the professional credentials to write a daily column on the weather for the *Hartford Courant*, something he did for 17 years. A longtime member of the faculty of Western Connecticut State University, and director emeritus of its weather center, Goldstein had a TV weather gig at WTNH-TV, and in 1999 authored "The Idiot's Guide to the Weather." Nominated for an Emmy for an educational series on the weather, he was described by a *Courant* staff writer as "an icon of Connecticut weather forecasting."

But when the Tribune Company merged with Times Mirror in 2000, it acquired the *Hartford Courant*, which had been a Times Mirror paper. And that marked the end of Dr. Mel's days as a daily weather columnist.

The media giant brought in Justin Kiefer of its Tribune-owned station and Fox affiliate, WTIC. Kiefer's column, adorned with a Fox 61 logo, was a part of Tribune's branding efforts, according to *Hartford Courant* columnist Roger Catlin. "Dr. Mel may have written a better column, but Kiefer took over because he's part of the Tribune family, like us," Catlin wrote in a column criticizing the FCC's proposed approval of newspaper-broadcast cross ownership in one market.

"Since the summer of 2000, when Tribune bought Times Mirror, readers and the newsroom have been adjusting to—sometimes struggling with—the new brand and affiliations, including those with WTIC, Channel 61," wrote *Courant* reader representative Karen Hunter in 2004. "The replacement of weather columnist Mel Goldstein with Channel 61's Justin Kiefer on the weather page was another Tribune cooperative effort that readers didn't care for but eventually stopped complaining about. Synergy is here to stay," Hunter concluded. "now, if only the tastes of *Courant* readers could be figured into the equation."

Ignoring Conflicts of Interest: The Milwaukee Story

The worst part about the huge conflict of interest scandal at the *Milwaukee Journal Sentinel* is that it was barely covered in Milwaukee. The state's largest newspaper failed to run any stories about the serious allegations concerning Robert Kahlor, the CEO and chairman of Journal Communications, which owned the *Milwaukee Journal* and *Milwaukee Sentinel* (which merged in 1995), as well as WTMJ-TV and WTMJ-AM, both ratings leaders for local news.

In 1994, Kahlor took on the high-profile and controversial position of chairman of the Milwaukee Stadium Commission, working to secure private and public financing for a baseball stadium. Kahlor was also one of four registered lobbyists working to promote the stadium on behalf of Journal Communications.

For Kahlor, who essentially controlled a huge chunk of Milwaukee's media outlets, to take this position on would have posed substantial questions about the ability of the Journal outlets to cover the stadium issue fairly. What made the issue even worse was the fact that WTMJ broadcast the games of the Milwaukee Brewers. So Journal Communications had a direct financial interest in saving baseball in Milwaukee.

Kahlor's actions . . . were troubling to many *Journal* reporters. "We were totally compromised at that point," Sue Ryon, deputy editor of the *Milwaukee Journal*'s editorial page, told *The Washington Post*. "We have no credibility. Anything we said, it was, 'Well, who can believe them? Look at the position they're in?' We felt as a newspaper, as an editorial board, handcuffed, and that was pretty much from the beginning."

But no Journal Communications outlets explored the conflict of interest question, or questioned the tenor of their coverage. Indeed, when Madison, Wisconsin's *Capital Times* dared to ask Kahlor about his media outlets' objectivity on the issue, he responded: "Quite frankly, this is the first time anyone's raised the question," conceding, however that coverage has "been positive. But it's been positive for the right reasons—because our reporters and editors understand that [a new stadium] is good for Wisconsin."

But the newspaper and its TV and radio outlets turned out to be more than handcuffed. "All four Journal media lost almost all objectivity," David Berkman, a retired mass communications professor and media columnist for Milwaukee's alternative weekly, told *Broadcasting and Cable* in 2001. "The Journal company's newspaper, TV-news shows and news-talk radio station all marched in lock-step supporting the public financing position," Beckman observed.

University of Wisconsin professor David Pritchard agreed. "We had two daily newspapers then, both owned by Journal Communications, one liberal, one conservative. They both ran front page editorials supporting the plan. The TV station fell in line. Even the very conservative talk show hosts on their radio station fell in line for a huge public subsidy."

There were virtually no dissenting voices in this debate. The other two TV stations largely supported the public financing argument. "[T]his case is a classic example of how a media monolith defeats the purposes of free and open debate. . . ."

"In this dynamic and competitive media landscape, a ban on cross-ownership simply makes no sense."

The Newspaper-broadcast Cross-ownership Ban Should Be Lifted

James L. Gattuso

The Federal Communications Commission (FCC) voted in December 2007 to relax the prohibition on media cross-ownership, allowing, under several guidelines, companies to own a newspaper and broadcast station in the same market. James L. Gattuso asserts in the following viewpoint that the FCC's decision is beneficial. He claims that as ailing newspapers are swamped by competing news sources on television and the Internet, cross-ownership can help them improve their offerings to consumers—such as enhancing local news—and remain viable and competitive. But the author proposes that the new rules have unnecessary limitations and prohibiting cross-ownership should be abolished. Gattuso is a senior research fellow at the Thomas A. Roe Institute for Economic Policy at the Heritage Foundation, a conservative public policy think tank.

James L. Gattuso, "The FCC's Cross-ownership Rule: Turning the Page on New Media," Heritage Foundation Backgrounder, May 6, 2008. Copyright © 2008 The Heritage Foundation. Reproduced by permission.

As you read, consider the following questions:

1. How does the author support his position that newspapers are in decline because of the Internet?

2. What anecdotal evidence does the author provide to back his claim that cross-ownership can encourage competition among news organizations?

3. According to Gattuso, what safeguards would prevent the forming of media monopolies if the cross-ownership prohibition was abolished?

Should radio and television stations be allowed to own newspapers? [In December 2007] the Federal Communications Commission (FCC) answered "sometimes." Specifically, the five-member agency voted to liberalize its 33-year-old blanket prohibition on cross-ownership, allowing broadcast licenses to be owned jointly with newspaper licensees.

The decision is now being challenged in Congress, where the Senate Commerce Committee recently approved a "resolution of disapproval" (Senate Joint Resolution 28) to overturn the FCC's action. Recent reports that publisher Rupert Murdoch, who purchased *The Wall Street Journal* last year, was trying to acquire Long Island's *Newsday* gave an added push to advocates of the ban. A full Senate vote is expected soon. [The Senate voted to block the ban on May 15, 2008.]

Critics of the FCC's action argue that newspaper/broadcast cross-ownership would lead to a dangerous concentration of power in the media business and warn of massive monopolies restricting Americans' access to news and varied information. Despite the apocalyptic rhetoric, however, Americans are in no danger of seeing their news and information monopolized, least of all by newspapers. Rather than increased concentration, recent decades have brought an historic expansion of information sources and their diversity. Instead of dominating today's media world, newspapers—and, to some extent, broadcasters—are struggling to remain viable.

In this dynamic and competitive media landscape, a ban on cross-ownership simply makes no sense. It is unnecessary and downright harmful to consumers—and even detrimental to competition. Moreover, like the FCC's long-repealed Fairness Doctrine, such rules can become a tool for ideologically motivated interference in media content.

The FCC was right to liberalize its cross-ownership rule. It would have been even better if the agency had repealed it altogether.

Decline of the Newspaper

The 21st century has not been kind to the newspaper. Long the predominant vehicle by which Americans received news and information, newspapers are now struggling to remain relevant—and financially viable—in a world of instant electronic mass communication. Simply put, few citizens today get their first or last news of the day from a bundle of paper tossed in the azaleas by a teenager on a bicycle.

The newspapers' dominance of information ended in the mid-20th century with the rise of radio and television broadcasting. Today, both media are being swamped by a tsunami of alternatives, ranging from 24-hour cable news channels to online news sites, wireless news alerts, and much more.

The news is grimmest for newspapers. Fewer than half of all Americans now read a newspaper every day, compared to 80 percent in 1950. Moreover, according to a Zogby poll released in February [2008], only 10 percent of adults say that newspapers are their primary source of news and information, compared to a whopping 48 percent who said that they rely most on the Internet. Broadcasters were also lagging, with 11 percent of American adults naming radio and 29 percent naming television as their primary news source.

Many of the top Internet news sites, of course, are operated by newspaper and broadcast companies, but they are far from dominant: Of the top 30 news Web sites, fewer than half are affiliated with traditional media firms, 11 of which are newspapers, or newspaper chains. Even the largest newspaper Web site—that of *The New York Times*—ranks only ninth.

Newspapers and broadcasters do retain more influence in certain information market subsets, particularly local news; but even there, consumers have significant choices. Cable and satellite services provide local news and information, as do many Web sites. There is also more newspaper-to-newspaper competition in the local sphere, with vibrant community papers and alternative weeklies providing local coverage in addition to major metropolitan dailies. Finally, in most medium and large cities, there is significant competition between broadcasters. Washington, D.C., for instance, has nine radio stations with news or talk formats; Baltimore has seven.

The decline of newspapers is clearly reflected in their ever-shrinking circulation and financial performance. Since 2001, paid newspaper circulation has fallen by 8.4 percent. Print advertising revenue, the lifeblood of most papers, is down even more, dropping by 9.4 percent [in 2007] alone. The same year, revenue from classified ads virtually collapsed, plummeting some 17 percent. Some of these losses were balanced by increased online advertising revenue, but overall losses still hit 7.9 percent.

The FCC's Decision

Recognizing this ongoing sea change in the media business, the FCC voted this past December [2007] to modify its 1975 ban on cross-ownership of newspapers and broadcast licensees. It was not a precipitous decision: The Commission had been studying and taking public comment on the issue for 11 years.

Nor was the change radical. Under the new rules, cross-ownership is still presumed to be contrary to the public interest in all but the 20 largest U.S. markets. Even in those markets, cross-ownership with a television station is presumed to be in the public interest only if the station is not one of the top four stations in a market and at least eight independently owned TV stations and major newspapers remain in the market (not counting Internet-only publications).

These initial presumptions may be rebutted by evidence that a particular deal is or is not in the public interest. The final decision is made on a case-by-case basis.

The FCC's modified rule does not open the doors for anyone to monopolize anything. Newspapers, for the most part, would be allowed to own or be owned by broadcasters only in markets larger than that of St. Louis. In these markets, concentration is hardly an issue. Eighteen of these 20 markets have at least 10 independently owned television stations, and 17 have at least two major newspapers. On average, they have some 70 independently owned radio stations.

Benefits of Reform

The new rule, however, does promise significant benefits for newspapers, broadcasters, and—most important—consumers. This is not just a matter of cutting costs: Joint ownership promises the ability to share news resources and expertise between print and over-the-air outlets. Reporting for a newspaper could be used, for instance, to provide information for news broadcasts, with video and audio footage supplementing print stories. Such cross-platform synergies are nothing new in the news business. Few news organizations today, for example, are without an online presence.

Joint ownership also can give the combined operation the resources to improve its offerings to consumers. This could benefit even local news, a particular area of concern for proponents of regulation. Three separate academic studies com-

Forestalling the Erosion

Without newspapers and their local news gathering efforts, we would be worse off. We would be less informed about our communities and have fewer outlets for the expression of independent thinking and a diversity of viewpoints. I believe a vibrant print press is one of the institutional pillars upon which our free society is built. In their role as watchdog and informer of the citizenry, newspapers often act as a check on the power of other institutions and are the voice of the people.

Allowing cross-ownership may help to forestall the erosion in local news coverage by enabling companies to share these local news gathering costs across multiple media platforms. . . . The revised newspaper/broadcast cross-ownership rule would allow a newspaper to purchase a broadcast station—but not one of the top four television stations—in the largest 20 cities in the country as long as 8 independent voices remain. This relatively minor loosening of the ban on newspaper/broadcast cross-ownership in markets where there are many voices and sufficient competition will help strike a balance between ensuring the quality of local news gathering while guarding against too much concentration.

Kevin J. Martin,
"Press Statement of Charmain Kevin J. Martin,"
December 18, 2007. www.fcc.gov.

missioned by the FCC found that television stations cross-owned with newspapers provided between 3 percent and 11 percent more local coverage than was provided by stand-alone TV stations.

Allowing such combinations could preserve competition in a market by allowing a struggling newspaper to keep up with a larger rival. There is anecdotal evidence, for example, that the cross-ownership ban decreased newspaper competition in the Washington, D.C., area. For decades, *The Washington Star* had served as a strong competitor to *The Washington Post*, aided—according to long-time WMAL-AM radio host Chris Core—by being under joint ownership with WMAL and WMAL-TV. But when FCC rules forced the sale of the radio station in 1977 and divestiture of the *Star* itself in 1978, the paper became a much weaker competitor, eventually folding in 1982.

Cross-ownership certainly is no panacea. Some industry observers are skeptical that the claimed synergies can be widely realized. And not every combination has been a success. In 2006, *The Washington Post* entered into a partnership with a local FM radio station to provide what it called "Washington Post Radio," a broadcast outlet for the *Post*'s news coverage, often featuring the newspaper's print staff. While such partnerships have worked elsewhere, in this case the two media cultures simply failed to mesh, and the venture was abandoned after about a year.

The possibility of failure, however, is no reason to ban such efforts: Few business strategies come with a guarantee of success. In fact, the risk of failure underscores the relative lack of market power held by newspapers, even those as large as *The Washington Post*.

Room for Improvement

The FCC's new rules are not perfect. The problem, however, is not that they liberalize too much, but that they don't liberalize enough. The limitation of newspaper-TV cross-ownership to the top 20 markets, for instance, is unnecessary, given the other safeguards that are provided. Of even more concern, the detailed rules provide only a "presumption" that any given combination is or is not in the public interest, leaving the FCC to make final determinations case by case.

The FCC states that these determinations will be based on very specific, objective factors. Debates over media ownership have often been driven by the content of media, not by their structure. Sometimes these are broad concerns—over the "proper" amount of local versus national news, for example. Often they are more specific, ideological concerns as to whether this or that cause is being covered and who is providing that coverage.

Much of the current media debate has been aimed at one individual: conservative publisher Rupert Murdoch. "Help Us Stop Rupert Murdoch," read an e-mail from the pro-regulation advocacy group Free Press hours after the Senate committee vote on S. J. Res. 28. Last year [2007], the same group co-authored (with the Center for American Progress) a report urging that the FCC tighten broadcast ownership caps into order to "correct" the alleged conservative bias in talk radio. This is exactly the sort of content issue in which the government should play no role.

Rather than keep the door open to such interference with content, the FCC would have done better to eliminate its cross-ownership rule completely. Media choice and competition would still be protected through well-established competition laws that are enforced by antitrust authorities.

Nevertheless, while the FCC should have gone farther, its rule changes are a small step in the right direction that recognizes the 21st-century realities of the newspaper business. The Senate should carefully consider the potentially harmful consequences of keeping in place ownership rules from the 20th century.

Periodical Bibliography

The following articles have been selected to supplement the diverse views presented in this chapter.

| Nikki Bannister | "Creating Our Own Opportunities in Communications," *Black Collegian*, April 2007. |

Leslie Cauley — "How We Pay for Cable May Be About to Change," *USA Today*, March 1, 2006.

Mark Fitzgerald — "Why Newspapers Will Lose on Media Cross-ownership," *Editor & Publisher*, November 2, 2006.

Nick Gillespie, Jesse Walker, and Drew Clark — "The Reluctant Planner," *Reason*, December 2004.

John M. Higgins and P.J. Bednarski — "How the Fight Over Indecency Threatens to Turn the Cable Industry Upside Down," *Broadcasting & Cable*, December 5, 2005.

Laura Horwitch — "Hollywood Versus the Big Six: Why Actors Should Care About Media Consolidation," *Back Stage East*, October 19, 2006.

Kathleen A. Kirby and Matthew L. Gibson — "The Newspaper-Broadcast Cross-ownership Rule: The Case for Regulatory Relief," *Communications Lawyer*, Spring 2007.

Eric Klinenberg — "Breaking the News," *Mother Jones*, March–April 2007.

David Lieberman — "View of Media Ownership Limits Changes," *USA Today*, January 29, 2007.

Kevin J. Martin — "Where's My Paper?" *International Herald Tribune*, November 15, 2007.

Robert McChesney and John Nichols — "Who'll Unplug Big Media? Stay Tuned," *Nation*, June 16, 2008.

OPPOSING
VIEWPOINTS®
SERIES

CHAPTER 3

How Does the Media Affect Society?

Chapter Preface

The "Bradley Effect" is a theory that attempts to explain inaccuracies and discrepancies in voter polls. It is named after the late Tom Bradley, an African American politician and former mayor of Los Angeles. In 1983, Bradley entered the election for California governor comfortably ahead in the polls and a heavily favored candidate. However, he lost to George Deukmejian, his white opponent. In reaction to the upset, some observers speculated that a segment of white voters who desired to appear racially unbiased lied and indicated that they would vote for Bradley in pre-election polls. The theory also is known as the "Wilder Effect," after African American politician Douglas Wilder; he won Virginia's 1989 gubernatorial race by a razor-thin margin despite his convincing lead in the polls. More recently, critics state that the Bradley Effect provides an explanation for the initially strong opposition to Proposition 8, the California gay marriage ban that passed in 2008. Also, some political analysts viewed president Barack Obama's leads in that year's Democratic primaries as deceptive when his then rival, Hillary Rodham Clinton, took New Hampshire.

Nonetheless, some skeptics do not believe that the Bradley Effect is a significant factor or even exists. Referring to the Los Angeles election that started it all, pollster V. Lance Tarrance contends that Deukmejian had an unaccounted edge over Bradley with early and absentee voters. Moreover, Nate Silver of the political Web site FiveThirtyEight.com declares in an August 2008 post that the Bradley Effect did not play a role in the 2008 race for the Democratic presidential nomination. "On the contrary," Silver maintains, "it was Barack Obama—not Hillary Clinton—who somewhat outperformed his polls on Election Day."

The Bradley Effect reveals the trepidation and cynicism that surrounds opinion polls. In the following chapter, experts and scholars investigate the potential effects mass media can have on the public.

| "The body of data has grown and grown and it leads to an unambiguous and virtually unanimous conclusion: media violence contributes to anxiety, desensitization, and increased aggression among children."

Media Violence May Cause Youth Violence

Hillary Rodham Clinton

In the following viewpoint excerpted from a speech she delivered to the Henry J. Kaiser Family Foundation, Hillary Rodham Clinton claims that pervasive media violence has a deleterious impact on the behavior of children. Clinton insists today's young viewers have hit a ceiling in terms of how much time they can spend absorbed in different types of media, and that violent content on television and the Internet, as well as in movies and video games, has been scientifically proven to increase aggression, anxiety, and desensitization. Therefore, in her opinion, media violence is a "silent epidemic" that encourages children to participate in a culture that condones aggression. Clinton is the U.S. Secretary of State and a former U.S. senator.

Hillary Rodham Clinton, "Senator Clinton's Speech to Kaiser Family Foundation Upon Release of Generation M: Media in the Lives of Kids 8 to 18," March 8, 2005.

As you read, consider the following questions:

1. According to Clinton, how much television does the average child watch?

2. How are children in the classroom different now compared with young students decades ago, in Clinton's view?

3. How does Clinton describe the impact of video game violence on children?

You know, I started caring about the environment in which children are raised, including the media environment, before my daughter was born, but then I began to take it very personally and in our own ways, Bill [former President Bill Clinton] and I tried to implement some strategies, some rules, some regulations but it wasn't quite as difficult 25 years ago as it is today. And although I confess, I still wonder what my daughter's watching as an adult, you know, those days of being involved in a direct and personal way are certainly over in my parenting experience.

But it is probably the single most commonly mentioned issue to me by young parents, almost no matter where I go, when we start talking about raising children. We start talking about the challenges of parenting today, and all of a sudden people are exchanging their deep concerns about losing control over the raising of their own children, ceding the responsibility of implicating values and behaviors to a multidimensional media marketplace that they have no control over and most of us don't even really understand because it is moving so fast we can't keep up with it. And so I've spent more than 30 years advocating for children and worrying about the impact of media. I've read a lot of the research over the years about the significant effects that media has on children. And I've talked and advocated about the need to harness the positive impacts that media can have for the good of raising, you know, healthy productive, children who can make their own way in this rather complicated world. And I've particularly advocated for trying to find ways to re-empower parents, to put them back in the driver's seat so they feel they are first knowledgeable and secondly in some sense helping to shape the influences that affect their children. . . .

And parents who work long hours outside the home and single parents, whose time with their children is squeezed by economic pressures, are worried because they don't even know what their children are watching and listening to and playing. So what's a parent to do when at 2 o'clock in the afternoon, the children may be at home from school but the parents aren't home from work and they can turn on the TV and both on broadcast and cable stations see a lot of things which the parents wish they wouldn't or wish they were sitting there to try to mediate the meaning of for their children. And probably one of the biggest complaints I've heard is about some of the video games, particularly Grand Theft Auto, which has so many demeaning messages about women and so encourages violent imagination and activities and it scares parents. I mean, if your child, and in the case of the video games, it's still predominantly boys, but you know, they're playing a game that encourages them to have sex with prostitutes and then murder them, you know, that's kind of hard to digest and to figure out what to say, and even to understand how you can shield your particular child from a media environment where all their peers are doing this.

And it is also now the case that more and more, parents are asking, not only do I wonder about the content and what that's doing to my child's emotional psychological development, but what's the process doing? What's all this stimulation doing that is so hard to understand and keep track of?

So I think if we are going to make the health of children a priority, then we have to pay attention to the activities that children engage in every single day. And of course that includes exposure to and involvement with the media.

And I really commend Kaiser [Family Foundation] for this report. It paints a picture that I think will surprise a lot of parents across the nation. It reveals the enormous diet of media that children are consuming, and the sheer force of the data in this report demands that we better pay attention and take more effective action on behalf of our children.

Media Is Omnipresent

Generation M: Media in the Lives of 8 to 18 Year Olds shows us that media is omnipresent. It is, if not the most, it is certainly one of the most insistent, pervasive influences in a child's life. The study tells us, as you've heard, on average that kids between 8 and 18 are spending 6.5 hours a day absorbed in media. That adds up to 45 hours a week, which is more than a full time job. Television alone occupies 3 to 4 hours a day of young people's time. And we all know, that in most homes, media consumption isn't limited to the living room, as it was when many of us were growing up. In two-thirds of kids' bedrooms you'll find a TV; in one-half you will find a VCR and/or video game console.

We also know from today's study that the incorporation of different types of media into children's lives is growing. . . . In one quarter of the time kids are using media, they are using more than one form at once. So, yes, they are becoming masters at multi-tasking. We know that the amount of time children are spending using media has not increased since the last Kaiser study.

So, today's study suggests that kids are in fact hitting a ceiling in terms of how much time they can spend with media. But they are using media more intensively, experiencing more than one type at the same time. And this creates not only new challenges for parents but also for teachers. I had a veteran teacher say to me one time, I said, "What's the differ-

Mimicking Aggressive Acts

Of great concern to early childhood educators is the negative effect of viewing violent programs on children's play. The importance of children's imaginative play to their cognitive and language development is well documented. Research demonstrates that watching violent programs is related to less imaginative play and more imitative play in which the child simply mimics the aggressive acts observed on television. In addition, many media productions that regularly depict violence also promote program-based toys, which encourage children to imitate and reproduce in their play the actual behaviors seen on television or in movies. In these situations, children's creative and imaginative play is undermined, thus robbing children of the benefits of play for their development. In their play, children imitate those characters reinforced for their aggressive behavior and rehearse the characters' scripts without creative or reflective thought. Children who repeatedly observe violent or aggressive problem-solving behavior in the media tend to rehearse what they see in their play and imitate those behaviors in real-life encounters.

National Association for the Education of Young Children,
"Media Violence in Children's Lives: A Position Statement of
the National Association for the Education of Young Children,"
April 1990.

ence between teaching today and teaching 35 years ago when you started?" And she said, "Well, today even the youngest children come in to the classroom and they have a mental remote controller in their heads. And if I don't capture their attention within the first seconds they change the channel. And it's very difficult to get them to focus on a single task that is frustrating or difficult for them to master because there's always the out that they have learned to expect from their daily interaction with media."

You know, no longer is something like the v-chip the "one stop shop" to protect kids, who can expose themselves to all the rest of this media at one time. And so parental responsibility is crucial but we also need to be sure that parents have the tools that they need to keep up with this multi-dimensional problem.

Of course the biggest technological challenge facing parents and children today is the Internet. And today's Kaiser Report goes a long way toward establishing how much media our children are consuming. And one thing we have known for a long time which is absolutely made clear in this report is that the content is overwhelmingly, astoundingly violent.

The Impact of Media Violence

In the last four decades, the government and the public health community have amassed an impressive body of evidence identifying the impact of media violence on children. Since 1969, when President [Lyndon] Johnson formed the National Commission on the Causes and Prevention of Violence, the body of data has grown and grown and it leads to an unambiguous and virtually unanimous conclusion: media violence contributes to anxiety, desensitization, and increased aggression among children. When children are exposed to aggressive films, they behave more aggressively. And when no consequences are associated with the media aggression, children are even more likely to imitate the aggressive behavior.

Violent video games have similar effects. According to testimony by Craig Anderson [director of the Center for the Study of Violence at Iowa State University] before the Senate Commerce Committee in 2000, playing violent video games accounts for a 13 to 22% increase in teenagers' violent behavior.

Now we know about 92% of children and teenagers play some form of video games. And we know that nine out of ten of the top selling video games contain violence.

And so we know that left to their own devices, you have to keep upping the ante on violence because people do get desensitized and children are going to want more and more stimulation. And unfortunately in a free market like ours, what sells will become even more violent, and the companies will ratchet up the violence in order to increase ratings and sales figures. It is a little frustrating when we have this data that demonstrates there is a clear public health connection between exposure to violence and increased aggression that we have been as a society unable to come up with any adequate public health response.

There are other questions of the impact of the media on our children that we do not know, for example, we have a lot of questions about the effect of the Internet in our children's daily lives.

We know from today's study that in a typical day, 47 percent of children 8 to 18 will go online. And the Internet is a revolutionary tool that offers an infinite world of opportunity for children to learn about the world around them. But when unmonitored kids access the Internet, it can also be an instrument of enormous danger. Online, children are at greatly increased risk of exposure to pornography, identify theft, and of being exploited, if not abused or abducted, by strangers.

According to the Kaiser study, 70% of teens between 15 and 17 say they have accidentally come across pornography on the web, and 23 percent report that this happens often. More disturbing is that close to one-third of teens admit to lying about their age to access a website. . . .

Standards and Values

Well this is a silent epidemic. We don't necessarily see the results immediately. Sometimes there's a direct correlation but most of the times it's aggregate, it's that desensitization over years and years and years. It's getting in your mind that it's okay to diss people because they're women or they're a different color or from a different place, that it's okay somehow to be part of a youth culture that defines itself as being very aggressive in protecting its turf. And we know that for many children, especially growing up in difficult circumstances, it's hard enough anyway. You know, they're trying to make it against the odds to begin with. . . .

So I think we have to begin to be more aware of what our children are experiencing and do what we can to encourage media habits that allow kids to be kids, and that help them to grow up into healthy adults who someday will be in the position to worry about what comes next in the media universe because we have no idea what parents in ten, twenty, thirty years will be coping with. All we can do is to try to set some standards and values now and then fulfill them to the best of our ability.

| "Concerns about media and violence rest on several flawed, yet taken-for-granted assumptions about both media and violence."

Media Violence Does Not Cause Youth Violence

Karen Sternheimer

Karen Sternheimer is a lecturer in the Department of Sociology at the University of Southern California. She also is author of Kids These Days: Facts and Fictions About Today's Youth *and* It's Not the Media: The Truth About Pop Culture's Influence on Children. *In the following viewpoint excerpted from* It's Not the Media, *Sternheimer proposes that the correlations between violence in mass media and youth violence are formed upon four flawed assumptions: the increase in media violence is creating more violent youths, children imitate media violence in deadly ways, young viewers cannot distinguish media violence from real violence, and research has proven the link between media violence and youth violence. She emphasizes the effects of other non-media factors, such as poverty and increasing violence rates in communities.*

As you read, consider the following questions:

1. How does the author support her claim that youth violence is in decline?

2. What is the main flaw of the "Bobo doll" study, in Sternheimer's view?

3. How does Sternheimer compare a scene with Wile E. Coyote and Road Runner, a scenario from *Law & Order*, and an incidence of gun violence at a party?

Media violence has become a scapegoat, onto which we lay blame for a host of social problems. Sociologist Todd Gitlin describes how "the indiscriminate fear of television in particular displaces justifiable fears of actual dangers—dangers of which television ... provides some disturbing glimpses." Concerns about media and violence rest on several flawed, yet taken-for-granted assumptions about both media and violence. These beliefs appear to be obvious in emotional arguments about "protecting" children. So while these are not the only problems with blaming media, this [viewpoint] will address four central assumptions:

1. As media culture has expanded, children have become more violent.

2. Children are prone to imitate media violence with deadly results.

3. Real violence and media violence have the same meaning.

4. Research proves media violence is a major contributor to social problems.

As someone who has been accused of only challenging the media-violence connection because I am secretly funded by the entertainment industry (which I can assure you I am not),

I can attest we are entering hostile and emotional territory. This [viewpoint] demonstrates where these assumptions come from and why they are misplaced.

Assumption #1: As Media Culture Has Expanded, Children Have Become More Violent

Our involvement with media culture has grown to the degree that media use has become an integral part of everyday life. There is so much content out there that we cannot know about or control, so we can never be fully sure what children may come in contact with. This fear of the unknown underscores the anxiety about harmful effects. Is violent media imagery, a small portion of a vast media culture, poisoning the minds and affecting the behavior of countless children, as an August 2001 *Kansas City Star* article warns? The fear seems real and echoes in newsprint across the country.

Perhaps an article in the *Pittsburgh Post-Gazette* comes closest to mirroring popular sentiment and exposing three fears that are indicative of anxiety about change. Titled "Media, Single Parents Blamed for Spurt in Teen Violence," the article combines anxieties about shifts in family structure and the expansion of media culture with adults' fear of youth by falsely stating that kids are now more violent at earlier and earlier ages. This certainly reflects a common perception, but its premise is fundamentally flawed: as media culture has expanded, young people have become *less* violent. During the 1990s arrest rates for violent offenses (like murder, rape, and aggravated assault) among fifteen- to seventeen-year-olds fell steadily, just as they did for people fourteen and under. Those with the highest arrest rates now and in the past are adults. Fifteen- to seventeen-year-olds only outdo adults in burglary and theft, but these rates have been falling for the past twenty-five years. In fact, theft arrest rates for fifteen- to seventeen-year-olds have declined by 27 percent since 1976 and the rates for those fourteen and under have declined 41 percent, while the arrest rate for adults has increased. Yet we seldom hear public outcry about the declining morals of adults—this complaint is reserved for youth. . . .

So why do we seem to think that kids are now more violent than ever? A Berkeley Media Studies Group report found that half of news stories about youth were about violence and that more than two-thirds of violence stories focused on youth. We think kids are committing the lion's share of violence because they comprise a large proportion of crime news. The reality is that adults commit most crime, but a much smaller percentage of these stories make news. The voices of reason that remind the public that youth crime decreased in the 1990s are often met with emotional anecdotes that draw attention away from dry statistics. A 2000 Discovery Channel "town meeting" called "Why Are We Violent" demonstrates this well. The program, described as a "wake-up call" for parents, warned that violence is everywhere, and their kids could be the next victims. Host Forrest Sawyer presented statistics indicating crime had dropped but downplayed them as only "part of the story." The bulk of the program relied on emotional accounts of experiences participants had with violence. There was no mention of violence committed by adults, the most likely perpetrators of violence against children. Kids serve as our scapegoat, blamed for threatening the rest of us, when, if anything, kids are more likely to be the victims of adult violence.

But how do we explain the young people who do commit violence? Can violent media help us here? Broad patterns of violence do not match media use as much as they mirror poverty rates. Take the city of Los Angeles, where I live, as an example. We see violent crime rates are higher in lower-income areas relative to the population. The most dramatic example is demonstrated by homicide patterns. For example, the Seventy-Seventh Street division (near the flashpoint of the 1992 civil unrest) reported 12 percent of the city's homicides in 1999, yet comprised less than 5 percent of the city's total population. Conversely, the West Los Angeles area (which includes affluent neighborhoods such as Brentwood and Bel Air) reported less than 1 percent of the city's homicides but accounted for nearly 6 percent of the total population. If media culture were a major indicator, wouldn't the children of the wealthy, who have greater access to the Internet, video games, and other visual media be at greater risk for becoming violent? The numbers don't bear out because violence patterns do not match media use.

Violence can be linked with a variety of issues, the most important one being poverty. Criminologist E. Britt Patterson examined dozens of studies of crime and poverty and found that communities with extreme poverty, a sense of bleakness, and neighborhood disorganization and disintegration were most likely to support higher levels of violence. Violence may be an act committed by an individual, but violence is also a sociological, not just an individual, phenomenon. To fear media violence we would have to believe that violence has its origins mostly in individual psychological functioning and thus that any kid could snap from playing too many video games. On-going sociological research has identified other risk factors that are based on environment: poverty, substance use, overly authoritarian or lax parenting, delinquent peers, neighborhood violence, and weak ties to one's family or community. If we are really interested in confronting youth violence, these are the issues that must be addressed first. Media violence is something worth looking at, but not the primary cause of actual violence. . . .

Assumption #2: Children Are Prone to Imitate Media Violence with Deadly Results

Blaming a perceived crime wave on media seems reasonable when we read examples in the news about eerie parallels be-

No Accurate Profile

The U.S. Secret Service intensely studied each of the 37 non-gang and non-drug-related school shootings and stabbings that were considered "targeted attacks" that took place nationally from 1974 through 2000. (Note how few premeditated school shootings there actually were during that 27-year time period, compared with the public perception of those shootings as relatively common events!) The incidents studied included the most notorious school shootings, such as Columbine, Santee and Paducah, in which the young perpetrators had been linked in the press to violent video games. The Secret Service found that there was no accurate profile. Only 1 in 8 school shooters showed any interest in violent video games; only 1 in 4 liked violent movies.

Lawrence Kutner and Cheryl K. Olson,
Grand Theft Childhood: The Surprising Truth
About Violent Video Games and What Parents Can Do.
New York: Simon & Schuster, 2008.

tween a real-life crime and entertainment. *Natural Born Killers, The Basketball Diaries, South Park,* and *Jerry Springer* have all been blamed for inspiring violence. Reporting on similarities from these movies does make for a dramatic story and good ratings, but too often journalists do not dig deep enough to tell us the context of the incident. By leaving out the non-media details, news reports make it is easy for us to believe that the movies made them do it.

Albert Bandura's classic 1963 "Bobo doll" experiment initiated the belief that children will copy what they see in media. Bandura and colleagues studied ninety-six children approximately three to six years old (details about community or economic backgrounds not mentioned). The children were divided into groups and watched various acts of "aggression" against a five-foot inflated "Bobo" doll. Surprise: when they had their chance, the kids who watched adults hit the doll pummeled it too, especially those who watched the cartoon version of the doll-beating. Although taken as proof that children will imitate aggressive models from film and television, this study is riddled with leaps in logic.

Parents are often concerned when they see their kids play fighting in the same style as the characters in cartoons. But as author Gerard Jones point out in *Killing Monsters: Why Children Need Fantasy, Super Heroes, and Make-Believe Violence*, imitative behavior in play is a way young people may work out pent-up hostility and aggression and feel powerful. The main problem with the Bobo doll study is fairly obvious: hitting an inanimate object is not necessarily an act of violence, nor is real life something that can be adequately recreated in a laboratory. In fairness, contemporary experiments have been a bit more complex than this one, using physiological measures like blinking and heart rate to measure effects. The only way to assess a cause-effect relationship with certainty is to conduct an experiment, but violence is too complex of an issue to isolate into independent and dependent variables in a lab. What happens in a laboratory is by nature out of context, and real world application is highly questionable. We do learn about children's play from this study, but by focusing only on how they might become violent we lose a valuable part of the data. . . .

Assumption #3: Real Violence and Media Violence Have the Same Meaning

Nestor Herrara's [an eleven-year-old boy who was killed by another eleven-year-old boy during a dispute in a movie theater in February 2001] accused killer watched a violent film; on that much we can agree. But what the film actually *meant* to the boy we cannot presume. Yet somehow press accounts would have us believe that we could read his mind based on his actions. It is a mistake to presume media representations of violence and real violence have the same meaning for audiences. Consider the following three scenarios:

1. Wile E. Coyote drops an anvil on Road Runner's head, who keeps on running;

2. A body is found on *Law and Order* (or your favorite police show);

3. A shooting at a party leaves one person dead and another near death after waiting thirty minutes for an ambulance.

Are all three situations examples of violence? Unlike the first two incidents, the third was real. All three incidents have vastly different contexts, and thus different meanings. The first two are fantasies in which no real injuries occurred, yet are more likely to be the subject of public concerns about violence. Ironically, because the third incident received no media attention, its details, and those of incidents like it, are all but ignored in discussions of violence. Also ignored is the context in which the real shooting occurred; it was sparked by gang rivalries which stem from neighborhood tensions, poverty, lack of opportunity, and racial inequality. The fear of media violence is founded on the assumption that young people do not recognize a difference between media violence and real violence. Ironically, adults themselves seem to have problems distinguishing between the two.

Media violence is frequently conflated with actual violence in public discourse, as one is used to explain the other. It is adults who seem to confuse the two. For instance, the *Milwaukee Journal Sentinel* reported on a local school district that created a program to deal with bullying. Yet media violence was a prominent part of the article, which failed to take into account the factors that create bullying situations in schools. Adults seem to have difficulty separating media representations from actual physical harm. Media violence is described as analogous to tobacco, a "smoking gun" endangering children. This is probably because many middle-class white adults who fear media have had little exposure to violence other than through media representations. . . .

Assumption #4: Research Conclusively Demonstrates the Link Between Media and Violent Behavior

We engage in collective denial when we continually focus on the media as main sources of American violence. The frequency of news reports of research that allegedly demonstrates this connection helps us ignore the real social problems in the United States. Headlines imply that researchers have indeed found a preponderance of evidence to legitimately focus on media violence. Consider these headlines:

"Survey Connects Graphic TV Fare, Child Behavior" (*Boston Globe*)

"Cutting Back on Kids' TV Use May Reduce Aggressive Acts" (*Denver Post*)

"Doctors Link Kids' Violence to Media" (*Arizona Republic*)

"Study Ties Aggression to Violence in Games" (*USA Today*)

The media-violence connection seems very real, with studies and experts to verify the alleged danger in story after story. Too often studies reported in the popular press provide no critical scrutiny and fail to challenge conceptual problems. In our sound-bite society, news tends to contain very little analysis or criticism of any kind.

The *Los Angeles Times* ran a story called "In a Wired World, TV Still Has Grip on Kids." The article provided the reader the impression that research provided overwhelming evidence of negative media effects: only three sentences out of a thousand-plus words offered any refuting information. Just two quoted experts argued against the conventional wisdom, while six offered favorable comments. Several studies' claims drew no challenge, in spite of serious shortcomings.

For example, researchers considered responses to a "hostility questionnaire" or children's "aggressive" play as evidence that media violence can lead to real-life violence. But aggression is not the same as violence, although in some cases it may be a precursor to violence. Nor is it clear that these "effects" are anything but immediate. We know that aggression in itself is not necessarily a pathological condition; in fact we all have aggression that we need to learn to deal with. Second, several of the studies use correlation statistics as proof of causation. Correlation indicates the existence of relationships, but cannot measure cause and effect. Reporters may not recognize this, but have the responsibility to present the ideas of those who question such claims.

This pattern repeats in story after story. A *Denver Post* article described a 1999 study that claimed that limiting TV and video use reduced children's aggression. The story prefaced the report by stating that "numerous studies have indicated a connection between exposure to violence and aggressive behavior in children," thus making this new report appear part of a large body of convincing evidence. The only "challenge" to this study came from psychologist James Garbarino, who noted that the real causes of violence are complex, although his list of factors began with "television, video games, and movies." He did cite guns, child abuse, and economic inequality as important factors, but the story failed to address any of these other problems.

The reporter doesn't mention the study's other shortcomings. First is the assumption that the television and videos kids watch contain violence at all. The statement we hear all the time in various forms—"the typical American child will be exposed to 200,000 acts of violence on television by age eighteen"—is based on the estimated time kids spend watching television, but tells us nothing about what they have actually watched. Second, in these studies, aggression in play serves as a proxy for violence. But there is a big difference between playing "aggressively" and committing acts of violence. Author Gerard Jones points out that play is a powerful way by which kids can deal with feelings of fear. Thus, watching the Power Rangers and then play-fighting is not necessarily an indicator of violence, it is part of how children fantasize about being powerful without ever intending to harm anyone. Finally, the researchers presumed that reducing television and video use explained changes in behavior, when in fact aggression and violence are complex responses to specific circumstances created by a variety of environmental factors. Nonetheless, the study's author stated that "if you . . . reduce their exposure to media you'll see a reduction in aggressive behavior." . . .

> *"For adolescents, exposure to alcohol ads is directly linked to subsequent drinking."*

Alcohol Advertising Encourages Teens to Consume Alcohol

RAND Corporation

The effects of alcohol advertising in the media on underage drinking is an area of social debate and scientific research. In the following viewpoint, the RAND Corporation asserts that its research avoids the pitfalls of previous studies and re-establishes a strong connection between alcohol advertising and underage drinking. According to RAND's findings, exposure to alcohol ads is directly linked to drinking in the mid-teens. RAND also states that awareness of beer brands occurs at an early age through viewing youth-oriented commercials. Therefore, the organization recommends that alcohol-advertising policies take youths' exposure and reactions into greater account. The RAND Corporation is a not-for-profit policy think tank based in Santa Monica, California.

As you read, consider the following questions:

1. In RAND's view, what are the kinds of influences of different alcohol ads on youths?

2. How can students in drug prevention programs learn to resist alcohol advertising, as stated by RAND?

3. According to RAND, at what age can children recognize specific beer ads on television?

Sales pitches for alcoholic beverages are everywhere: at the grocery store, in magazines, on television, and at concession stands. Kids can't avoid them, even though alcohol ads are supposedly aimed at adults. Researchers have long suspected a connection between alcohol advertisements and underage drinking, but positive correlations to date may have been due to other factors like peer and family influences that affect both drinking and ad exposure.

Researchers with the RAND Corporation have now made a much stronger connection, taking a new look at alcohol ads and youth drinking with studies designed to avoid the pitfalls of earlier ones. Furthermore, they tested to see if participation in a school-based drug prevention program can counteract the impact of alcohol ads.

Their key findings: For adolescents, exposure to alcohol ads is directly linked to subsequent drinking, but different kinds of ads have different influences depending on a youngster's prior alcohol use. Even in elementary school, kids recognize certain alcohol advertisements. School drug prevention programs can help blunt the impact of alcohol ads on youth.

Alcohol Advertising Does Influence Youth Drinking

For two different studies, the RAND researchers analyzed data from thousands of Midwestern students participating in a large-scale field trial of drug prevention curricula known as Project ALERT (for middle schools) and ALERT Plus (for middle schools and high schools). The curricula were developed by the RAND Corporation.

The studies reported here focused on beer advertisements because beer ads are more pervasive than those for other kinds of alcohol, and the ads are more likely to appear where young people might see them.

In the first study, adolescent health experts Phyllis Ellickson and Rebecca Collins tracked exposure to beer ads and subsequent drinking among more than 3,000 students as they moved from middle school to high school. Data for this study came from three different questionnaires the students filled out: a baseline drinking survey at the start of grade 7, a survey about alcohol advertising and TV viewing at the end of grade 8, and a survey about past-year drinking at the end of grade 9.

The study divided students into two groups:

- Initial nondrinkers: grade 7 students who said they had never tried alcohol, not even a sip (39 percent).

- Initial drinkers: grade 7 students who said they had already tried alcohol (61 percent).

The study examined four venues of beer advertising: magazines, concession stands, grocery/convenience stores, and TV. Students were asked how often in the past year they had read specific magazines and saw specific televised sports and late-night programs that account for a majority of TV alcohol ads seen by adolescents. These had been selected with input from student focus groups and advertising tracking data. Students were also shown photographs of typical beer displays at concession stands and in grocery stores and asked to estimate how often in the past year they had seen something similar.

Findings on Influence of Alcohol Ads

Exposure to alcohol ads is directly linked to subsequent drinking in mid-adolescence.

- Nearly half of the 7th grade nondrinkers became drinkers by 9th grade.

- More than three-quarters of the 7th grade initial drinkers had used alcohol during 9th grade.

- The more ads youth saw during 8th grade, the greater the likelihood they fell into one of these two groups of 9th grade drinkers.

The ad effect is real. It persisted after the researchers accounted for numerous other influences on youth drinking, for example, doing poorly in school or having peers who drink. "That, plus looking at changes in drinking over time, is what makes this study stronger than most of those done in the past," said Ellickson.

Different kinds of ads have different influences on youth depending on a youngster's prior alcohol use.

- For initial *nondrinkers*, in-store beer displays had the most sway.

- For initial *drinkers*, ads in magazines and concession stand displays at sports and music events had the most influence.

"It appears that a combination of drinking experience and venue influences adolescent responses to advertising," said Ellickson. "Advertising that links alcohol with everyday life, such as supermarket displays, appears to have more influence on drinking initiation. On the other hand, kids who are already drinkers appear to pay more attention to ads in more-sophisticated venues—at sports and music events or in magazines like *Playboy* and *Rolling Stone.*"

School Drug Prevention Programs Can Dampen the Appeal of Alcohol Ads

The RAND researchers also found that a prevention curriculum that helps youth identify and resist alcohol marketing strategies can counteract the effect of some ads on adolescent drinking.

About half of the students in the advertising study were enrolled in ALERT Plus, an evidence-based drug prevention program that adds high school lessons to the original Project ALERT middle school program now used in all states. Lessons help students recognize different forms of alcohol marketing, identify persuasive appeals, and counter pressures to use alcohol, cigarettes, and marijuana. For example, students learn about product placement in venues like supermarkets and movies as well as how to rewrite advertising messages to tell the real truth about alcohol use.

The study found that students who took part in the ALERT Plus program were less likely than the control students to drink in 9th grade. Furthermore, the ALERT Plus students who hadn't started drinking before the lessons began were less susceptible to the persuasive appeals of in-store advertisements.

"This is the first time we have seen that a school drug prevention program like ALERT Plus can counteract the pro-drinking effect of at least some types of alcohol advertising," said Ellickson.

Awareness of TV Ads Starts Early

In the study described above, the RAND researchers found some evidence that viewing beer ads on TV encourages the nondrinkers to start drinking. However, the link was not as strong as that for advertising in magazines, at concession stands, and with in-store displays. "It may be that the real effect of television advertising only shows up after repeated exposure over many years. And elementary school children may

Low Income and Minority Groups as Targets

Alcohol advertisers target minority groups. Researchers have found that alcohol advertising is disproportionately concentrated in low-income minority neighborhoods. One study found that minority neighborhoods in Chicago have on average seven times the number of billboards advertising alcohol as do Caucasian neighborhoods. Such concentration of alcohol advertising and availability likely translates into increased problems associated with alcohol use in these communities.

American Academy of Family Physicians,
"Alcohol Advertising and Youth (Position Paper)," 2004.
www.aafp.org.

be more vulnerable to the persuasive appeals of TV ads than adolescents," according to the RAND researchers.

The possibility of a delayed effect of TV alcohol ads on youth drinking ties in with results from a second RAND study on alcohol advertising and its impact on youth. For this study, Collins and Ellickson assessed survey responses from fifteen hundred 9th grade students taking part in the ALERT Plus field test and two thousand 4th grade students from elementary schools in the same districts. The RAND team found that younger children watch a lot of TV and see lots of alcohol ads. In this study, 4th graders were exposed to an average of 376 TV beer ads over a seven-month period while the older teenagers were exposed to 286. This difference reflected that the elementary school children watched nearly twice as many televised professional sports programs, where beer is heavily advertised, than did their teen counterparts.

One way to learn whether children actually pay attention to ads that they see on TV is to measure ad awareness or recognition. The RAND researchers did this, finding that kids recognize specific beer ads on TV at an early age, at least as young as age 9.

The researchers had asked the students to respond to a set of photographs from four TV beer commercials that aired frequently during the six months before the survey. The photographs were edited to remove any indication of the product and the brand. They included a youth-oriented nationally aired beer ad featuring an animated ferret and lizards, along with three other beer ads with more adult appeal. For comparison, the researchers also showed students edited photographs from an ad for a product that is more appropriate for youth—a popular soft drink commercial featuring a young girl.

Findings on Alcohol Advertising Awareness

- *Ad awareness*. Most students in both age groups reported seeing the animated ferret and lizards ad, a level of ad awareness that was not far behind that of the youth-marketed soft drink ad. In contrast, less than a quarter reported seeing the more adult-oriented beer ad, even though it was aired when comparatively more youth were watching TV.

- *Brand recognition*. Nearly 80 percent of 9th graders knew the ferret and lizards ad well enough to correctly name the brand of the beer. Even one in three of the 4th graders could also do so. More than half of the 4th graders and 85 percent of the 9th graders could name the brand of the soft drink ad. Only around 10 percent of both groups could name the brand of the more adult-oriented beer ad.

The study also found that more than one in four 4th graders could name three or more brands of beer, and an equal number knew the slogan for at least one brand.

"While the younger children were less familiar with the TV beer ads, less interested in them, and liked them less, our results suggest there is cause for concern regarding this group," said Collins. "The average fourth grader knows a lot about beer ads and brands for someone ten years under the legal drinking age."

Policy Implications

The 2003 Institute of Medicine's report, *Reducing Underage Drinking: A Collective Responsibility*, estimates the social cost of underage drinking at $53 billion, including $19 billion from traffic accidents and $29 billion from violent crime. Combating underage drinking involves multiple approaches. With regard to alcohol advertising, the RAND studies described in this [viewpoint] raise the following issues for policymakers to consider:

Alcohol Advertising Policy

- Alcohol advertising policy should take into consideration all ad venues to which adolescents are exposed, including magazines, TV, in-store displays, and concession stands at sports events and concerts.

- Given the high rates of beer advertising awareness among adolescents watching televised sports, the current practice of airing frequent beer ads during such programming warrants examination.

- Youth reactions to specific ads should be examined on a regular basis, by advertisers and by policymakers, so that ads particularly appealing to young people can be identified and pulled.

Future Research

- Future research should focus on identifying ways to counter the impact of "special venue" advertising on youth who have already started drinking.

- More studies are needed to understand the impact of television advertising on underage drinking, specifically by targeting the possible cumulative effect of exposure to TV alcohol ads year after year.

School Drug Prevention Programs

- Helping children become aware of and able to counter the multiple sources of alcohol advertising to which they are exposed should be an important component of school prevention programs.

| *"In short, there is no evidence that alcohol ads target underage persons."*

Alcohol Advertising Does Not Encourage Teens to Consume Alcohol

David J. Hanson

David J. Hanson is professor emeritus of sociology of the State University of New York at Potsdam, and he is a noted alcohol and drinking expert. In the following viewpoint, Hanson refutes allegations that alcohol advertising targets teens. He maintains that the findings of the Center on Alcohol Marketing and Youth (CAMY) are not backed by science, disputing CAMY's claims that beer and liquor campaigns in magazines and on television, the radio, and the Internet encourage underage drinking. Instead, Hanson suggests that the objectives of alcohol advertising are to appeal to established consumers, strengthen brand loyalty, and increase a company's share of the market.

As you read, consider the following questions:

1. How does Hanson argue against CAMY's assertion that alcohol advertising in magazines is directed toward youths?

2. How does the author support his claim that alcohol advertising does not affect consumption or abuse?

3. According to Hanson, how is "normalizing" alcohol through advertising beneficial?

The Center on Alcohol Marketing and Youth (CAMY) was established and its activities funded by the Pew trusts and the Robert Wood Johnson Foundation, a ten *billion* (not million) dollar ($10,000,000,000.00) organization. The stated mission of CAMY is to monitor "the marketing practices of the alcohol industry to focus attention and action on industry practices that jeopardize the health and safety of America's youth." It seeks to create "public outrage" against alcohol advertising to achieve its objective.

CAMY begins with an assumption which it then sets out to prove. In doing so it is clearly an activist group rather than an objective scientific organization seeking to learn the truth. Judging from CAMY's statements and activities, it's doubtful if the Center would ever find any alcohol advertising or any marketing practice to be acceptable. This may be an example of the Burger King phenomenon: Pew and Johnson pay for the research and "have it their way."

CAMY Rejects Scientific Procedure

The Center on Alcohol Marketing and Youth distributes its reports without peer review, contrary to the way real science operates. In peer review, an editor or other neutral person submits the report to a number of peer experts in the subject of the research. These authorities read the report to determine if it meets the minimum standards for research. By examining the adequacy of the research methods, the statistical analyses performed, the logic of the analysis, and other essential criteria, approval by peer experts reduces the chances that the findings are erroneous.

The Center on Alcohol Marketing and Youth is "a new anti-alcohol group that has launched a 'crusade' against alcohol advertising."

—*The Wall Street Journal*

Peer review is fundamental to science. Without it, there is absolutely no reason to have any confidence in the findings of a report. Peer review is the major mechanism science uses to maintain quality control. It's a fundamental defense against incompetence, quackery, pseudo-science, and downright dishonesty.

Without peer review, an advocacy group report full of erroneous and misleading statistics can be passed off to the public as a scientific report. That's exactly what the Center on Alcohol Marketing and Youth does.

Alcohol Advertising in Youth-Oriented Magazines

Out of Control: Alcohol Advertising Taking Aim at America's Youth—A Report on Alcohol Advertising in Magazines, by the Center on Alcohol Marketing and Youth, suggests the CAMY itself may be out of control.

CAMY asserts that a large proportion of alcohol ads appear in "youth-oriented" magazines. Presumably a youth-oriented magazine would be one directed primarily to youthful readers. At a minimum, it would appear that a majority of the readers of a youth-oriented magazine would have to be youths. Such a magazine would have at least 51% youth readers, but perhaps it should be two-thirds, three-fourths, or some higher proportion to be considered youth-oriented.

Not according to the Center on Alcohol Marketing and Youth. If it defined "youth-oriented magazine" as generally understood by most people, it wouldn't have sensationalist, headline-grabbing statistics to report. Instead CAMY defines a youth-oriented magazine as one whose youthful readership is over 15.8%! That's right, anything over a mere 15.8%.

Not a single so called youth-oriented magazine examined by CAMY has a majority of youth readers. Nor does a single one have even close to a majority of youth readers.

CAMY: Alcohol Industry "Targets" Underage Youths

CAMY repeatedly asserts that alcohol producers "target" underage persons with their advertising in magazines and other media. CAMY's logic and study method actually *defines* targeting as advertising in any magazine or other outlet with an adolescent exposure of over 15.8%.

Enter the Statistical Assessment Service (STATS) at George Mason University, an independent organization that examines science issues in the news. STATS explains that CAMY's logic is that "a magazine that appeals to more youth than the population average is one that alcohol companies *would avoid* if they weren't 'targeting' youth."

That logic requires some questionable assumptions and leaps of faith. And, of course, it's impossible to direct ads to those age 21–30 without younger readers also seeing the ads. An alternative approach is to examine *empirically* the factors that alcohol companies use in selecting magazines for ad placements.

This has been done by Dr. Jon Nelson, Emeritus Professor of Economics at Pennsylvania State University and the findings published in *Contemporary Economic Policy*. Prof. Nelson identified factors that might affect advertising decisions, such as the cost of the ads, the circulation of the magazine, the proportion of readers under the age of 21, sales outlets, the subject matter of the magazine, and demographics of the readership such as race and income.

STATS points out that, according to Dr. Nelson's research, "the proportion of young readers among the readership did not make much difference. The influential factors were the size of the audience (not just how many people bought the magazine, but how many actually read it), and how much an ad costs per 1,000 copies in circulation."

In short, there is no evidence that alcohol ads target underage persons.

Alcohol Advertising on Radio

CAMY's report, *Radio Daze: Alcohol Ads Tune In Underage Youth*, asserts that those aged 12 to 20 hear more alcohol beverage ads than do those age 21 and older. However, an analysis has revealed that CAMY's own data suggest that the advocacy group has overstated the exposure of young people to alcohol ads on radio by a whopping five hundred percent (500%).

In reality, it appears that, at most, 17 percent of alcohol beverage ads on radio are heard by those under age 12–20. . . .

Alcohol Advertising on Television

CAMY's report, *Television: Alcohol's Vast Adland*, will disturb anyone who values intellectual honesty. This political advocacy document transforms a speculative suggestion by the Federal Trade Commission (FTC) into an assertion that "research clearly indicates" that alcohol ads lead young people to drink. In reality, neither the scientific evidence nor the FTC statement indicates any such thing.

CAMY then reports some irrelevant studies in a futile attempt to prove that alcohol ads make teenagers drink. However, CAMY's evidence is so very weak that even a student in an introductory research methods course should be able to see through this attempted deception.

Worse yet,

> The rest of CAMY's evidence is even lamer: kids' familiarity with the Budweiser frogs, surveys in which people express the opinion that ads make drinking more appealing, and a statement by the National Association of Broadcasters that

"radio and television audiences, particularly kids" like "clever jingles, flashy lights, fast talking, and quick pacing." The pathetic thing is that you have to assume CAMY is making the strongest case it can.

The scientific evidence simply doesn't support CAMY's agenda. That's why it resorts to anecdotes, distortions and even misrepresentations in order to try to convince people.

Alcohol Advertising on the Internet

In *Clicking with Kids: Alcohol Marketing and Youth on the Internet*, CAMY attempts to create public outrage. To do so, it by plays outrageously fast and loose with the facts.

- CAMY is distressed that citizens under the age of 21 can visit web sites sponsored by alcohol beverage companies. It ignores the fact that people of any age can visit grocery stores that, in most states, sell beer and wine.

- CAMY implies that the existence of video games on some alcohol sites means that they are intended to lure underage visitors. It ignores the fact that the average age of those who play video games is 29.

- CAMY protests that there is no adult supervision of those visiting alcohol web sites. It ignores the fact that there is no adult supervision of any sites on the internet other than that provided by parents and guardians.

- CAMY charges that the web sites are "cyber playgrounds" for underage people. It ignores that fact that those under the age of 21 are not disproportionately visitors to the sites.

- CAMY suggests that the sites violate the alcohol industries' own advertising and marketing standards. It ignores the well-known fact that research by the Federal

Trade Commission leads it to conclude that the content of the sites is directed to adults, not underage persons.

- CAMY implies that minors are enticed and victimized by the sites. It ignores the fact that the only people under the age of 21 who can visit the sites are those who misrepresent their age—that is, these so-called victims have to be liars.

- CAMY complains about underage visitors being "immersed in beer and liquor marketing." It ignores the fact that scientific research concludes that alcohol ads don't cause non-drinkers to become drinkers.

- CAMY implies that the FCC [Federal Communications Commission] disapproves of such web sites as a danger to young people. It again ignores the fact that the Federal Trade Commission concludes that the content of the alcohol sites is directed to adults, not underage persons.

- CAMY calls for a federal threat of censorship. It ignores the fact that the United States Constitution protects the free speech rights of those who post web sites.

And, unfortunately, the list goes on. . . .

Frogs and Former Presidents

Much has been made by many anti-alcohol activists of the fact that young people often have greater recognition of some alcohol brand labels and promotional characters than of former U.S. presidents. These reports make good headlines but what does it all mean? Probably nothing because there is absolutely no evidence that such recognition leads to experimentation, consumption, or abuse of alcohol. Sometimes it even appears to be related to less drinking later.

Similarly, most adults are probably much better at identifying photos of popular entertainers than of William Henry

Harrison, Franklin Pierce, Chester Arthur, John Tyler, or other former presidents of the U.S. But that doesn't mean they've been seeing too many alcohol beverage commercials.

The Impact of Alcohol Advertising

The definitive review of scientific research from around the world has found that advertising has virtually no influence on consumption and no impact on either experimentation with alcohol or its abuse. This is consistent with other reviews of the research literature.

A study by the Federal Trade Commission found that there is "no reliable basis to conclude that alcohol advertising significantly affects consumption, let alone abuse."

A United States Senate subcommittee reported in the *Congressional Record* that it could not find evidence to conclude that advertising influences non-drinkers to begin drinking or to increase consumption.

The United States Department of Health and Human Services in a report to Congress concluded that there is no significant relationship between alcohol advertising and consumption. Therefore, it did not recommend banning or imposing additional restrictions on alcohol advertising.

The founding Director of the National Institute on Alcohol Abuse and Alcoholism has pointed out that "There is not a single study—not one study in the United States or internationally—that credibly connects advertising with an increase in alcohol use or abuse."

There is clear consensus in the scientific community that alcohol advertising does not lead non-drinkers to begin drinking, does not increase the consumption of alcohol, and does not lead to alcohol abuse.

What Advertising Does

If advertising doesn't increase consumption, why bother to advertise? The answer is simple: to increase market share.

Alcohol is what economists call a "mature" product category in that consumers are already aware of the product and its basic characteristics. Therefore, overall consumption is not affected by advertising specific brands.

Instead of increasing total consumption, the objective of advertisers is to encourage consumers to switch their brand and create brand loyalty. Thus, effective advertisers gain market share at the expense of others, who lose market share. They do not try to increase the total market for the product. An example can illustrate why they don't.

Assume that the total retail value of beer produced annually is $50 billion. If a producer's advertising campaign increases its 10% market share by one percent, its sales would increase by $500 million. However, if the total market for beer increased by one percent, the brand with a 10% market share would only experience a sales increase of $50 million.

Clearly, a producer has a great incentive to increase market share, but little incentive (and no ability) to increase the total market. For this reason, advertisers focus their efforts on established consumers. They seek to strengthen the loyalty of their own customers and induce other customers to try their brand.

Normalizing Alcohol

A common anti-alcohol argument against alcohol beverage advertising is that it "normalizes" drinking in the minds of young people. To the extent that this is true, the ads may be performing a positive role in society.

The commonplace nature of alcohol ads helps beverage alcohol be viewed as another mundane consumer product, right alongside aspirin, cookies, and alkaline batteries. This is a constructive way for young people to view alcohol beverages.

On the other hand, if we treat beverage alcohol as a dangerous substance to be avoided and not even advertised, we inadvertently raise it up from the ordinary into the realm of the mysterious, highly desirable, tantalizing, must-have Big Deal. In so doing, we slip into the familiar, failed pattern of demonizing the substance of alcohol and making it more desirable to underage persons.

We should help young people regard the substance of alcohol as neutral—neither inherently good nor inherently bad. What matters is how it is used, and we must convey by word and example that the abuse of alcohol is never humorous, acceptable, or excusable. And its abuse is not a sign of adulthood or maturity.

Do alcohol ads portray the products being enjoyed in the most appealing settings and by the most attractive people? Of course they often do—no less than do ads for cars, instant coffee and anti-fungal sprays. That normalcy of alcohol ads helps demystify the product—which is a good place to begin encouraging realistic, moderate, and responsible attitudes about it.

Responsible attitudes toward alcohol are based on the understanding that such beverages are yet another part of life over which individuals have control, like exercise, personal hygiene, or diet.

If alcohol beverages are to be used moderately by those adults who choose to consume them, then it is important that these beverages not be stigmatized, compared to illegal drugs, and associated with abuse. They aren't dangerous poisons to be hidden from sight and become a subject of mystery and perhaps fascinating appeal. But that would be the message if alcohol ads are banned or kept from the view of young people. . . .

Parents Are Highly Influential . . . Alcohol Ads Are Not

The Center on Alcohol Marketing and Youth uses bright graphics, colorful charts, and assertive language in attempting to persuade. But the scientific fact is that alcohol commercials do not cause young people to drink. The greatest influence of their beliefs, attitudes and behaviors is actually from their parents.

Parents are much more influential than they generally realize. For example, among six things that might affect their decisions about drinking, 66% of American youth aged 12 to 17 identified their parents as a leading influence:

- Parents (66%)

- Best friends (26%)

- Teachers (12%)

- What they see on television (8%)

- What they see in ads (6%).

It is parents, rather than alcohol ads, with the great influence over the alcohol decisions of young people.

Periodical Bibliography

The following articles have been selected to supplement the diverse views presented in this chapter.

Michael Barone	"Are the Polls Accurate?" *Wall Street Journal*, October 22, 2008.
Michael S. Jellinek	"Children Living in a Violent World," *Pediatric News*, January 2007.
Peter Katel	"Debating Hip-hop: Sex and Violence," *CQ Researcher*, June 15, 2007.
Jeffrey Kluger	"Hollywood's Smoke Alarm," *Time International*, April 30, 2007.
Stephen Marche	"Are Things Getting a Little Violent? A Thousand Words About Our Culture," *Esquire*, August 2008.
Patricia Moore	"The Kids Are Alright: Advertising to Children and Teenagers Is Emotive, Sensitive, and Risky—But the Rewards Can Be Counted in the Billions," *AdMedia*, July 2008.
Kevin J. O'Brien	"Magazine Publishers See Future, But No Profit, in Shift to Internet," *International Herald Tribune*, March 18, 2007.
Mega Pelligrini	"Little Stomachs, Big Power: The Restaurant Industry Is Appealing to Children Through Menu Choices, Advertising, and Promotions," *National Provisioner*, June 2007.
Andrew Saloman	"A Collision Over Violence: As More FCC Regulation Looms, Debate Rages Over Freedom and Responsibility," *Back Stage East*, April 19, 2007.
Greg Schneiders	"Political Polls Aren't Perfect, But Are Far From Meaningless," *PR Week*, August 27, 2007.

CHAPTER 4

How Will the Media Be Affected by the Internet?

Chapter Preface

According to the Audit Bureau of Circulations, while single-copy magazine sales fell 11 percent in the second half of 2008 from the previous year, subscriptions rose 0.5 percent. Yet, Associated Press business writer Anick Jesdanun, on Yahoo.com in February 2009, proposes that the upside is not reassuring in the long haul. "[T]he drop in single-copy sales translates to less revenue because publishers typically make more from newsstand sales than from subscriptions, which are sold at a discount but help publishers boost circulation totals to lure advertisers." These sales, Jesdanun continues, are "particularly vulnerable" during recessions because they are "impulse buys" at kiosks and checkout lines.

Along with the recent slew of folding publications such as *CosmoGirl* and *Electronic Gaming Monthly*, and the continued success of such Web sites as *Pitchfork* and the *Huffington Post*, the future of magazines is uncertain in a digital age. To adapt, migration to the Internet is becoming the norm; numerous monthlies are going quarterly and shifting focus to online content. But in an April 2007 *Independent* article, titled "The Slow Death of the Magazine," journalist Ian Reeves insists that digital advertising revenues will never match that of print. "[A]dvertisers just won't pay you anywhere near the same amount, no matter how many mouse clicks you can show them, than they will for a lovingly-printed spread," he contends. Furthermore, publishing on the Internet may not be lucrative. According to *New York Times* writer Kevin J. O'Brien in a March 2007 *International Herald Tribune* article, "The economics of online publishing, though lower-cost because no paper or printing is used, are still daunting . . . because most Internet-savvy readers expect online text to be free."

The evolution of the disposable magazine into a high-concept, premium publication may hint at the shape of things to come in the industry. For instance, *BusinessWeek* columnist Jon Fine speculated in December 2007 that *Monocle* (which costs $150 for a yearly subscription and is printed on a variety of paper stock) may have a fighting chance. He notes, "[I]t cherishes the primacy of a print publication as physical object. . . . *Monocle* is either prescient, or steering sharply toward an audience that doesn't exist." Others believe the medium is not dying, no matter the format. Simon Wear, chief operating officer of Future Publishing, declares in a March 2009 post by Alex Lockwood on Online Journalism Blog, "The future of magazines is glorious. Both print and online." If, he advises, a publication does not try to compete as a software company and caters to niche interests.

The rise of Web 2.0—citizen journalism, blogging, social networking, user-generated content—is still unfolding. Whether it will transform or hasten the death of magazines and other print publications remains to be seen. In the following chapter, the authors discuss the implications of technological advancement on mass media.

> "The endgame for newspapers is in sight."

The Internet Will Make Newspapers Obsolete

Philip Meyer

Philip Meyer is the retired Knight chair of journalism at the University of North Carolina. He also is the author of The Vanishing Newspaper: Saving Journalism in the Information Age. *In the following viewpoint, Meyer argues that Internet use is hastening the demise of the old newspaper business model. Meyer asserts the paperless Web's speed and low cost of operation allow new, innovative publishers, in better and cheaper ways, to accomplish what newspapers have done previously. He predicts that surviving newspapers will focus on retaining valuable community influence and the trust of its core audience of educated, opinionated readers.*

As you read, consider the following questions:

1. When does the author predict the zero point of newspaper readership?

2. What characteristics will a surviving newspaper have, as stated by Meyer?

Philip Meyer, "The Elite Newspaper of the Future," *American Journalism Review*, October-November 2008. Reproduced by permission of *American Journalism Review*.

3. How are Henry Ford and Craig Newmark similar, in the author's view?

The endgame for newspapers is in sight. How their owners and managers choose to apply their dwindling resources will make all the difference in the nature of the ultimate product, its service to democracy and, of course, its survival.

In an article in the December 1995 issue of *AJR* [*American Journalism Review*] called "Learning to Love Lower Profits," I predicted the financial turbulence that we are seeing today. The piece urged stakeholders in newspaper companies to accept the inevitability of lower returns and to apply their resources to maintaining their community influence.

A decade later, I marshaled the evidence for that strategy in a book titled *The Vanishing Newspaper: Saving Journalism in the Information Age*. The argument was quantitative and complex. Judging by the Google alerts the book's title has accumulated since then, readers took away the wrong message.

This reference from *The Economist* is typical: "In his book 'The Vanishing Newspaper,' Philip Meyer calculates that the first quarter of 2043 will be the moment when newsprint dies in America as the last exhausted reader tosses aside the last crumpled edition."

That's a clever image, and it is true that extrapolating the recent linear decline in everyday readership would show a zero point in April 2043. But newspaper publishers are not so relentlessly stubborn that we can expect them to continue churning out papers until there is only one reader left. The industry would lose critical mass and collapse long before then.

Moreover, straight-line trends do not continue indefinitely. Nature throws us curves. Even the daily-reader chart showed the barest suggestion of a leveling off in the 1980s before resuming its downward march.

Recently, I took another look at the readership data from the General Social Survey of the National Opinion Research

Center at the University of Chicago and tried a different metric. Reasoning that you could still make a pretty good business from an audience reading less than daily, I tracked the percentage of adults who reported reading a newspaper at least once a week. That chart, from 1972 to 2002, shows a much clearer leveling off in the 1980s. Then, at the end of the decade, as though somebody blew a whistle and ordered a column-right march, the line snakes downward again.

Acting on a hunch, I got newsroom census data from the American Society of Newspaper Editors. In 1978, when the census began, daily newspapers had 43,000 news/editorial workers. Their number grew until peaking at 56,900 in 1990, after which an irregular decline set in. That temporary growth in staffing corresponds neatly with the temporary halt in the readership decline of the 1980s. Having more people to put more things in the paper kept more people reading.

After 1990, of course, the effects of the Internet kicked in. When writing *The Vanishing Newspaper*, I underestimated the velocity of the Internet effect. It is now clear that it is as disruptive to today's newspapers as [inventor Johannes] Gutenberg's invention of movable type was to the town criers, the journalists of the 15th century.

The town crier's audience was limited to the number of people who could be assembled within the range of an unamplified human voice. Printing changed everything. It made the size of the audience theoretically limitless and, by the creation of multiple records, enabled more reliable preservation of knowledge.

Wrecking the Old Newspaper Business Model

The Internet wrecks the old newspaper business model in two ways. It moves information with zero variable cost, which means it has no barriers to growth, unlike a newspaper, which has to pay for paper, ink and transportation in direct proportion to the number of copies produced.

And the Internet's entry costs are low. Anyone with a computer can become a publisher, as [news editor] Matt Drudge demonstrated when he broke the Monica Lewinsky story in 1998 [exposing Lewinsky's affair with President Bill Clinton] and countless bloggers have shown in the decade since. These cost advantages make it feasible to make a business out of highly specialized information, a trend that was under way well before the Internet.

Way back in 1966, sociologist Richard Maisel reported on it at the annual conference of the American Association for Public Opinion Research in Swampscott, Massachusetts. Since World War II, specialized media had been enjoying more growth than general media. It was true across all platforms. Quarterly magazines, with their limited audiences, did better than monthly magazines, which did better than weekly magazines. Community papers grew more than metropolitan papers. The effect was visible even in New York theater. Off-Broadway productions, with their smaller theaters and more specialized content, were growing more than those on Broadway.

Postwar newspapers met the specialization challenge fairly well for a while. A metropolitan newspaper became a mosaic of narrowly targeted content items. Few read the entire paper, but many read the parts that appealed to their specialized interests. I still remember a fellow Navy trainee in 1953, when the Korean War was on. He religiously bought the newspaper every day. Instead of looking for the war news, he worked the crossword puzzle and threw the rest of the paper away. "Crossword puzzles," he said. "That's all newspapers are good for." Newspaper marketing since then has stressed ways to optimize the selection of pieces for that mosaic of such highly specific interests.

Sending everything to everybody was a response to the Industrial Revolution, which rewarded economies of scale. The model became less and less efficient as printing technology improved and made more specialized publications feasible. At the same time, retailing became more specialized, with boutiques squeezing out the big department stores. Specialized advertisers discovered that they could get mailing lists to target their most likely customers with tailored appeals and high-quality printing. Newspapers matched their printing quality with slick-paper inserts, but that did not solve the targeting problem.

Robert Picard, a media economist who looks at newspapers from an international perspective, believes that they try to do too much. He expressed this view in June [2008] at the Carnegie-Knight Task Force conference on the Future of Journalism at Harvard University. Newspapers "keep offering an all-you-can-eat buffet of content, and keep diminishing the quality of that content because their budgets are continually thinner," he said. "This is an absurd choice because the audience least interested in news has already abandoned the newspaper."

If they should peel back to some core function, newspapers would still have to worry about the Internet and its unbeatable capacity for narrowcasting. The newspapers that survive will probably do so with some kind of hybrid content: analysis, interpretation and investigative reporting in a print product that appears less than daily, combined with constant updating and reader interaction on the Web.

Anyone Can Play

But the time for launching this strategy is growing short if it has not already passed. The most powerful feature of the Internet is that it encourages low-cost innovation, and anyone can play. I am ashamed to admit that *The Vanishing Newspaper* contains no mention of Craig Newmark. The significance

In Any Other Industry

In any other industry, a product that lost 1 percent of market share for two decades—only to then double or triple that rate of decline—would be declared dead. The manufacturer would discontinue it and rush out a replacement product more in line with the desires of the marketplace. So, let's finally come out and say: Newspapers are dead. They will never come back. By the end of this decade, the newspaper industry will suffer the same death rate—90-plus percent—that every other industry experiences when run over by a technology revolution.

Michael S. Malone,
"Silicon Insider: Newspaper Nearing Death?"
abcnews.go.com, March 24, 2005.

of craigslist is not just that it uses the Internet but that it empowers public-spirited motivation. Newmark is what business school people call a "bad competitor" because he appears more interested in serving society than making money.

He does make money by charging certain kinds of users, but the bulk of his service is free. He is like Henry Ford who, after introducing the Model T [in 1908], lowered prices, increased wages and concentrated on market share rather than maximizing profit. When challenged by shareholders unhappy that their dividends weren't higher, he replied that they should view his company as "an instrument of service rather than as a machine for making money."

Craigslist and more specialized online classified ad sites could not have appeared at a worse time for newspapers, which were becoming increasingly dependent on classified advertising. In keeping with the broad trend toward specialization, classified ads moved from 18 percent of newspaper advertising revenue in 1950 to 40 percent in 2000.

The lesson to take away from craigslist is that we should be prepared to be surprised yet again. There are other Craig Newmarks out there, waiting for their hour. Some will be on the news-editorial side, figuring out new, better and cheaper ways to do what newspapers have traditionally done. Newspapers can try to beat them to the good ideas, but, as Harvard's Clayton Christensen has noted, the very qualities that made companies succeed can be disabling when applied to disruptive innovation. Successful disruption requires risk taking and fresh thinking.

On the other hand, it is possible to envision a scenario in which newspapers trim down to a specialized product and survive by serving a narrow market well. They are already trimming down. But what are they trimming down to? Have they thought about what's left after all the shrinkage?

A Newspaper's Most Important Product

One of the rules of thumb for coping with substitute technology is to narrow your focus to the area that is the least vulnerable to substitution. Michael Porter included it in his list of six strategies in his book *Competitive Advantage: Creating and Sustaining Superior Performance.* The railroads survived the threat from trucks on Interstate highways and airlines by focusing on the one thing they could still do better: moving bulk cargo across long distances.

What·service supplied by newspapers is the least vulnerable?

I still believe that a newspaper's most important product, the product least vulnerable to substitution, is community influence. It gains this influence by being the trusted source for locally produced news, analysis and investigative reporting about public affairs. This influence makes it more attractive to advertisers.

By news, I don't mean stenographic coverage of public meetings, channeling press releases or listing unanalyzed collections of facts. The old hunter-gatherer model of journalism is no longer sufficient. Now that information is so plentiful, we don't need new information so much as help in processing what's already available. Just as the development of modern agriculture led to a demand for varieties of processed food, the information age has created a demand for processed information. We need someone to put it into context, give it theoretical framing and suggest ways to act on it.

The raw material for this processing is evidence-based journalism, something that bloggers are not good at originating.

Not all readers demand such quality, but the educated, opinion-leading, news-junkie core of the audience always will. They will insist on it as a defense against "persuasive communication," the euphemism for advertising, public relations and spin that exploits the confusion of information overload. Readers need and want to be equipped with math-based defenses.

Newspapers might have a chance if they can meet that need by holding on to the kind of content that gives them their natural community influence. To keep the resources for doing that, they will have to jettison the frivolous items in the content buffet.

The best publishers have always known that trust has economic value. In *The Vanishing Newspaper*, I reported that advertising rates increased by $3.25 per Standard Advertising Unit (SAU) for each one percentage point increase in the persons who said they believed what they read in the paper. And papers with higher trust were more successful in resisting the long-term decline in household penetration. Both of these results were based on a limited sample, newspapers in communities tracked by the John S. and James L. Knight Foundation. Since most of them were former Knight Ridder papers, the overall quality was pretty high. A more representative sample would have higher variance in quality and could show a stronger effect.

Retaining Newspaper's Core

Won't democracy be endangered if the newspaper audience shrinks down to this hard core? Not at all. As far back as 1940, the sociologist Paul Lazarsfeld discovered that voters get their information from one another as much as from direct consumption of the media. He called this the "two-step flow" from opinion leaders to the general public. The Internet is enhancing that two-step flow, converting it to a many-step flow. The problem is not distributing the information. The problem is maintaining a strong and trusted agency to originate it. Newspapers have that position of trust in the minds of the public.

Another piece of the endgame should be bolstering whatever community papers are part of a newspaper company's strategy. A community paper benefits from a very important kind of specialization. Sadly, as staffs shrink, I don't see that happening.

There is some good news about investigative reporting: Nonprofits are turning out to be an impressive source of support. This development is not as radical as it sounds. Even at the peak of their earning power, newspapers relied on federally recognized charities for much of their staff training. My own reporting career at Knight Ridder included examples of charity and government support for investigations into the social issues of the 1960s and 1970s.

Nonprofit-financed investigative operations like ProPublica and the Center for Public Integrity might lead to a demonstration effect for local philanthropists. Mixing profit and nonprofit motivations might be awkward, but ProPublica's cooperation with "60 Minutes" for its maiden effort was an encouraging start. Replicating that kind of teamwork at a local level with local nonprofits and local papers is an intriguing possibility.

But it won't be a worthwhile possibility unless the newspaper endgame concentrates on retaining newspapers' core of trust and responsibility. The mass audience is drifting away, and resources should be focused on the leadership audience. If existing newspapers don't do it, new competitors will enter their markets and do it for them.

| "Newspapers have . . . important assets that none of the digital newcomers even pretend to match."

The Internet Will Not Make Newspapers Obsolete

Bill Keller

In the following viewpoint excerpted from his memorial lecture at Chatham House in London, Bill Keller counters the view that newspapers will not survive as the Internet becomes a greater media presence. Although digital tools allow readers to easily access, customize, and share news and other media, Keller asserts that newspapers provide a product that cannot be replaced by lesser sources. He states that unlike search engines, newspapers have skilled reporters working globally and on location. Another clear advantage, Keller claims, is that newspapers follow and are held to a rigorous set of standards of fairness and accuracy. Keller is executive editor of the New York Times.

As you read, consider the following questions:

1. According to the author, how is reporting in Bagdad an example of "extreme" journalism?

2. What are the four tenets of journalism, as stated by Keller?

3. How does Keller describe the future of the *New York Times*?

My assignment tonight is to talk about the state of newspapers in America. No doubt you have read that newspapers, at least in my country, are beleaguered. That is undeniable. Let me count the ways.

To begin with, we have endured [eight] years of the most press-phobic government in a couple of generations. I don't intend to blame the plight of the newspaper business on [former President] George [W.] Bush. He did not invent our great disrupter, the internet. (That, you recall, was [former Vice President] Al Gore.) The Bush administration has merely fed a current of public antipathy that has been running against us for a long time, a consequence of our own failings and, perhaps, a tendency to blame the messenger when news is bad. . . .

And then there is the business of our business. As has been widely reported, many daily newspapers are staggering from an exodus of subscribers, a migration of advertisers to the web, and the rising costs of just about everything. Newspapers are closing bureaus and hollowing out their reporting staffs.

At places where editors and publishers gather, the mood these days is funereal. Editors ask one another, "How are you?" in that sober tone one employs with friends who have just emerged from rehab or a messy divorce.

A journalism professor at the University of North Carolina, named Philip Meyer, has done some studies about the decline of American newspaper readership. His extrapolation of the data shows that, if newspapers do nothing to change their ways, they will lose their very last reader in the year 2044. In October, if you want to mark your calendars.

On the stock exchanges, the value of newspaper shares has declined. Of the dwindling number of quality titles in the US, several are being bought up by new owners who seem completely free of nostalgia for the idea of journalism as a public trust. . . .

Newspapers Will Survive

For all of the woes besetting our business, I believe with all my heart that newspapers—whether they are distributed to your doorstep, your laptop, your iPhone or a chip implanted in your cerebral cortex—will be around for a long time. Newspapers, including at least a few very good newspapers, will survive, simply put, because of that basic law of market economies: supply and demand. The supply of what we produce is sadly diminishing. And the demand has never been greater. . . .

And I would argue that in this clattering, interconnected, dangerous world, journalism that cuts through the noise has never been needed more. We have a war going very badly in Iraq, and another one in Afghanistan where our declaration of victory looks very premature. We have nuclear Pakistan on the brink of chaos. We have an America whose standing in the world is at low ebb. We have a global terror threat that makes us wish for the simple enmities of the Cold War—although anyone who follows Russia these days has to think, be careful what you wish for. We have, at last, a consensus that our climate is warming at a dangerous pace. North Korea has joined the club of nuclear nations, and Iran seems determined to follow. Technology and demographics have rocked the foundations of many industries (not just my own). We have new leadership in Britain, France and Germany, among other places. In America we have the most interesting presidential campaign since at least 1968—possibly the first campaign with more candidates than voters. We have Darfur. [President of Venezuela] Hugo Chavez. China and India.

In other words, something is happening out there, and if we don't understand it, it's not just the newspaper business that is in peril.

And at this time of desperate need for reliable news reporting, the supply is dwindling.

That may sound like a strange thing to say in the age of 'too much information'. You turn on your computer and there is a media tsunami: blogs, Google News, RSS feeds [rich site summary feeds, a format for delivering regularly changing Web content], social sites like MySpace and file-sharing programs like YouTube. You can harvest it from around the world. You can customize it. You can have it delivered to your cell phone. You know where many thousands of younger readers go these days to follow breaking news stories? They go—or at least they are sent by search engines—to Wikipedia, an online, communal encyclopaedia written and edited by well, essentially written and edited by any passerby who wants to log on and contribute. . . .

It is certainly true that technology has lowered the barriers to entry in the news business. The old joke that freedom of the press belongs to the man who owns one is now largely inoperative. Freedom of the press now belongs to anyone with an Internet Service Provider. This is all unsettling to the traditional news business, but it is also an opportunity. In an easy-entry business, success goes to those who—and here you must supply those ironic quote marks—move up the value chain. That is, you succeed by offering something of real value that the newcomers cannot match.

Journalists in the Field

As it happens, newspapers have at least two important assets that none of the digital newcomers even pretend to match. One is that we deploy worldwide a corps of trained, skilled reporters to witness events and help our readers understand them. This work is expensive, laborious, sometimes unpopular, and occasionally perilous.

The *New York Times* has six correspondents assigned to Iraq, plus a rotating cast of photographers, plus Pentagon correspondents who regularly travel with the troops. We employ, in addition, about 80 brave Iraqis—many of them handpicked stringers based in towns that are no longer safe for westerners. Sustaining the Baghdad bureau costs several million dollars a year. We take extraordinary precautions to keep our people safe, but two of our Iraqi colleagues have been murdered in cold blood, almost certainly because they worked for an American organisation. . . .

Baghdad is an extreme example of the retrenchment in journalism, but it is not an isolated one. Survey the newsrooms of America and you will find that in most places foreign bureaus have been cut or eliminated—this in the time of globalisation. You will find that Washington bureaus have been squeezed and consolidated, that election coverage has been hollowed out by staff cuts and buyouts—this at a time when American politics is going through a period of profound upheaval.

The civic labour performed by journalists on the ground cannot be replicated by legions of bloggers sitting hunched over their computer screens. It cannot be replaced by a search engine. It cannot be supplanted by shouting heads or satirical television shows.

What is absent from the vast array of new media outlets is, first and foremost, the great engine of newsgathering—the people who witness events, ferret out information, supply context and explanation.

Google News and Wikipedia don't have bureaus in Baghdad, or anywhere else. With a few exceptions, they do not, in the cold terminology of the 21st-century media business, create content. Wikipedia's policy actually forbids original material; it is a great mash-up of secondary sources. Wikipedia and Google aggregate information from, well, from us. From the *Times*, from the *Guardian*, and from a lot of less dependable sources. They can pool reporting from hundreds of news outlets but what if there aren't hundreds of news outlets? Or what if many of them are simply unreliable? And how would you know? Here's an experiment you can perform at home: If you are inclined to trust Google as your source for news, Google yourself.

I am a convert to blogs, those live, ad-libbed, interactive monologues that have proliferated by the millions, with an average audience consisting of the blogger and his immediate family. The *Times* actually produces more than 30 of them, in which our reporters muse on subjects ranging from soccer to health to politics. Blogs can swarm around a subject and turn up fascinating tidbits. They allow you to follow a story as it unfolds. And, yes, there are bloggers who file first-hand reports of their experiences from distant places, including Iraq— and sometimes their work is enlightening or intriguing. But most of the blog world does not even attempt to report. It recycles. It riffs on the news. That's not bad. It's just not enough. Not nearly enough. . . .

So, our first and most important advantage is that we have journalists in the field. And the other is that we have a rigorous set of standards. We have a code of accuracy and fairness we pledge to uphold, a high standard of independence we defend at all costs, and a structure of editorial supervision to enforce our standards.

The Tenets of Journalism

I want to digress for a few minutes to state some basic tenets of journalism, or at least the kind of journalism we aim to practice at the *New York Times*. What I'm about to say is taken as a given by most people who work in the serious news media in America, yet it is regarded by many people outside our business with suspicion verging on disbelief. Even with audiences like this one, who are presumed to be well read and world-savvy, I'm constantly surprised by the presumption of bad faith when people talk about our business. That is in some measure the fault of our own shortcomings, the well-publicised examples of journalistic malfeasance, the episodes of credulous reporting in the prelude to the war in Iraq, the retreat of some news organisations from serious news into celebrity gossip, and so on. It also reflects the fact that we live in cynical times, in a clamorous new media world of hyperventilating advocacy. And so I always feel obliged to pause and state what, to me and many of you, is obvious. . . .

First: We believe in a journalism of verification rather than assertion, meaning we put a higher premium on accuracy than on speed or sensation. When we report information, we look hard to see if it stands up to scrutiny. Now, of course, newspapers are written and edited by humans. We get things wrong. The history of our craft is tarnished down the centuries by episodes of partisanship, gullibility, and blind ignorance on the part of major news organisations. (My own paper pretty much decided to overlook the Holocaust as it was happening.) And so there is a corollary to this first principle: when we get it wrong, we correct ourselves as quickly and forthrightly as possible. . . .

Second on my list of precepts is this: We believe in transparency—that is, we aim to tell you how we know what we know, to attribute our information as much as possible to named sources, to rely on documentary evidence when we can. When we need to protect our sources, which is often necessary to bring you information powerful people don't want you to know, we should explain why we regard the information as credible, and whether the source has an axe to grind. As my math teacher used to say, we show our work.

Third, we are agnostic as to where a story may lead; we do not go into a story with an agenda or a pre-conceived notion. We do not manipulate or hide facts to advance an agenda. We strive to preserve our independence from political and economic interests, including our own advertisers. We do not

A Distinct Product

[N]ewspapers are continuing to take advantage of tools offered to them by new technology. The use of online tools such as video, podcasts, and blogs supplements the information readers can obtain in a printed newspaper and helps publications evolve away from the "online repository" format—where newspaper websites provide regurgitated story content from print editions—and move toward a more full-featured model of news. Because these tools enhance user experiences and provide value beyond just written material, newspaper websites are beginning to evolve beyond their printed counterparts and become a distinct product in their own right. The continuation of this trend will be positive for newspapers, which will benefit from an environment that can accommodate both print and online news.

Bivings Group, "American Newspapers and the Internet: Threat or Opportunity?" July 19, 2007. www.bivingsreport.com.

work in the service of a party, or an industry, or even a country. When there are competing views of a situation, we aim to reflect them as clearly and fairly as we can. . . .

Finally, on my short list of precepts: We don't do this as a hobby but as a career. Whether you call it a craft, or a profession, or an occupation, it is something we take seriously, and we demand levels of training and experience that we seek to pass on from one generation to the next.

In short, to sum up this little detour through the protocols of American-style journalism, our mission is not to tell readers what we think or what they are supposed [to] think, but to supply them, as best we can, the basis to make up their own minds. . . .

A Good Bit of Life Left

The truth is, people crave more than raw information. What they crave, and need, is independent judgment, someone they can trust to vouch for the information, dig behind it, and make sense of it. The more discerning readers want depth, they want scepticism, they want context, they want the material laid out in a way that honours their intelligence, they might even welcome a little wit and grace and style.

The newspaper companies that will offer these things 20 years from now will be different, even more different than today's newspapers are from the newspapers of 20 years ago. We are already changing before your eyes, morphing into hybrid newsrooms that produce journalism in print and on-line, and racing to invent enough revenue from our growing websites to compensate for the diminishing returns in print.

I can't draw you a neat map from our current predicament to this new destination. Indeed, I would regard with deep suspicion anyone who claims to have such a map. [British philosopher] Isaiah Berlin famously divided the intellectual world into foxes and hedgehogs—the hedgehog knows one big thing, the more promiscuous fox leaps from idea to idea. The internet is a fox medium, that's fox with a lower case 'f'. It is perilous to get locked too firmly into one big idea—that people will pay for content on the web, or that they won't; that the key to success is brand loyalty, or, on the contrary, that it's all about scale. Anyone who gets too declarative about this medium is likely to be hedgehog road kill. But while I can't tell you quite when, or quite how, we reach the Promised Land, I will offer up a few reasons for my optimism that we will get there.

First, the printed newspaper has a good bit of life left in it, and that buys us time. The *New York Times*, that loveable old-fashioned bundle of ink and cellulose, is still a profitable undertaking. We sell more than a million copies a day, more than a million and a half on Sunday, and included in those numbers is a large pool of loyal subscribers who stick with us through controversy and price rises. I expect they will tide us over nicely until the digital revenues rise enough to keep us afloat. The printed newspaper may eventually become a cult product, like vinyl LP records, but we are some years from that day.

And the people who bring you high-quality newspapers turn out to be rather adaptable and entrepreneurial. Newspapers, including my own, have periodically reinvented themselves, adding features, revising formats, redefining markets. At the moment, we are demonstrating a good deal of agility in tapping the potential of web journalism. The *Guardian* is an excellent example of this, and so is my paper. Two years ago we began merging the staff of our website, who are mostly young and mostly not raised in the church of mainstream journalism, into the newsroom of ageing, technologically challenged hacks like myself. I won't pretend this has been a marriage entirely free of quarrels and misunderstandings, but with some counselling the newlyweds have discovered a bedrock of common interest and mutual respect. The collaboration of high journalistic standards and engineering proficiency has produced quite an explosion of creative energy. . . .

The web is also ideal for tapping into our audience, drawing them into the political conversation, and even using them to help us gather the news. When former Senator John Edwards announced this summer that he intended to continue his campaign after his wife was diagnosed with an advanced case of cancer, we were naturally curious to know how voters would respond. We noticed that the comments posted on our website by readers reacting to the news included many extraordinarily personal and thoughtful messages from families that had faced similar choices. That pool of comments became the starting point for a follow-up story that was unusually rich. More recently we have inaugurated what amounts to an online focus group of undecided voters. We plan to follow them through the campaign and engage them in regular conversations about the candidates and issues.

It may seem paradoxical, but this medium that seems so immediate and transitory—because it is also cumulative and almost boundary-less—allows us to serve readers a depth and breadth of coverage far greater than we could offer in print. It is, I think, an antidote to the superficiality of a modern political campaign.

By the way, if you'll forgive one more slight detour: as much as I revel in our increasing mastery of web journalism, it is not entirely clear to me that what we are now inventing on the web, nytimes.com, or Guardian Unlimited, will replace the newspaper as we know it. There is something tremendously appealing about a portable, authoritative package of dispatches from all corners of the world, from all corners of the culture, selected and written for you by intelligent people. That, I think, helps explain the continuing popularity of a weekly magazine like the *Economist,* or the *Week,* which I think of as Economist Lite. Turning the pages of a newspaper or a news magazine also offers a reader serendipitous encounters that are hard to replicate in the quicker, reader-driven format of a website. It's the difference between a clock and a calendar. Maybe, just maybe, our websites will continue evolving into what they will become, and the newspaper will simultaneously take on a digital form of its own—something you read like a newspaper, but on a portable tablet or a sheet of electronically charged plastic. That, too, is something we are looking into.

The Gravest Danger

So, my confidence in our future depends on the continuing vitality of the printed paper, the entrepreneurial energy we have unleashed at our website, but above all it depends on one other thing. While some newspaper companies are cutting the heart out of their core business, our company continues to invest in it. At least twice in my lifetime the *New York Times* has seemed to be on the verge of extinction—once, during the New York City financial crisis of the mid-1970s, and again during the deep national recession of the late 1980s. Both times my paper resisted the temptation to panic. It invested in new things, it adapted, and it flourished. I believe that this time, too, newspapers that stay true to their mission will endure. In the end, I believe the gravest danger to the future of newspapers is not a hostile administration in Washington, not the acid rain of criticism, not a business model upended by new technology, it is a loss of faith, a failure of resolve on the part of the people who make newspapers.

| "Magazines and papers should consider blogging to build their legitimacy in targeted communities and societies."

Blogs Are an Innovative Part of Journalism

Patrick Baltatzis

In the following viewpoint, Patrick Baltatzis declares that blogging and its innovations are assets to journalism. Baltatzis contends that blogs provide a valuable resource for journalists, a goldmine of news ideas, leads to potential stories, and feedback. The author also proposes that magazines and newspapers can use blogs to reach and build legitimacy in targeted communities and niche audiences. Furthermore, he adds, compared with print, blogging is a low-investment, low-risk enterprise. Baltatzis is a reporter in Sweden and was a 2006 Innovation Journalism Fellow at Stanford University.

As you read, consider the following questions:

1. How does the author approach the debate of whether blogging is journalism?

2. What is Lawrence Lessig's view of blogging?

3. How did blogs contribute to Baltatzis's story on Pay-Pal?

At a meeting [in fall 2005] discussing innovation journalism, the editor-in-chief of Sweden's monthly publication *Axxess* tried to describe innovation journalism. He suggested that it is a matter of quality—good vs. bad journalism, not a genre with its own methodology and characteristics. He asserted that innovation journalism is a professional pursuit using known approaches, techniques and skills.

David Nordfors, founder of the Innovation Journalism program, said that traditional media has structural problems. He argued that innovations cover different beats, and that traditional newsrooms cannot handle the style of 'broadband' coverage that supposedly is required by innovation journalism.

If Innovation Journalism is good journalism, not only in style and expression, but also in its effort to dig deeper and broaden its scope and perspectives, how is quality conceived and achieved in an environment of abundant, transitional and complex information? What qualities, skills and tools are required to assimilate, digest and then distribute relevance and meaning where attention is more valued than most physical goods? How does new media technology fit into all this? How do RSS-feeds [rich site summary-feeds, also known as "really simple syndication," a format for delivering regularly changing Web content] and easy web-publishing tools (which have contributed to the growth of the blog) and podcasts contribute to interesting stories, good journalism and the future of publishing?

These are relevant questions in these times of change and transition, when new publishing technologies are challenging the very nature of journalism. . . .

The Ubiquitous Question

Journalism, and free press committed to honoring journalism, enables different interests to participate and have an active voice in such power plays. Journalism prospers via reader and democratic advocacy. Hopefully, publishing houses also prosper.

But development of network-communications technologies, governed by Moore's law [which states that the number of transistors on a chip doubles every 24 months, has been the guiding principle of the high-tech industry since it was coined by Intel co-founder Gordon Moore in 1965], challenges traditional media and newsrooms with new formats and new players. What has been valid for 400 years, since [inventor Johannes] Gutenberg's invention [of a printing press with moveable type] and introduction of the mass reproduction of ideas, is now up for grabs via innovation—low-cost reproduction and instant distribution. Time-consuming print and audio journalism must compete in this environment.

"My worst competitor is not another magazine. It is readers attention and time," said Josh Quittner, editor-in-chief of *Business 2.0*.

My assertion is that papers and magazines must create new value to maintain readerships if they are to continue to play a pivotal role in society.

One way is to approach and empower readers and create deeper relationships with them. Blogging is a promising concept and a new channel of special interest to publishers, as is podcasting. The latter will not be dealt with in detail in this [viewpoint], but the same reasoning applies.

"Just because you're a media publisher doesn't mean that you should be in all media," said Quittner. Innovation Journalism trying to get acceptance in newsrooms can benefit from the emergence of blogs and contribute to a needed paradigm in publishing and journalism.

Ongoing debate questions whether blogging is journalism. Though an interesting topic—sometimes blogs are journalism, sometimes not—I will not contribute to that debate here.

The ubiquitous question in this [viewpoint] is this:

How can concepts such as blogging and podcasting be assets for reporters and writers in a journalistic endeavor (covering different beats)?

To answer this question, I've interviewed journalists who are blogging and their editors-in-chief, and searched the net for interesting perspectives on the subject.

What Is Blogging?

Emerging technologies converging into new ones

The blog is a publishing innovation, a digital newswire that, due to the proliferation of the Internet, low production and distribution costs, ease of use and really simple syndication (RSS), creates a new and powerful push-pull publishing concept. As such, it changes the power structures in journalism, giving yesterday's readers the option of being today's journalists and tomorrow's preferred news aggregators.

The roaming of ideas

Blogging is a concept whereas publishing text on the web is combined with its syndication. Users or other bloggers subscribe to these syndication feeds (RSS-feeds), which automatically appear on the subscriber's website, blog or in a newsreader.

"The central virtue of blogging, I've decided, is that in the proverbial agora, or online marketplace of ideas, bloggers are like Socrates on speed," wrote Chris Mooney, the 2005 winner of the Scientific American's Science and Technology Web award.

Though Mooney calls the blogosphere a marketplace, blogging is also the roaming—as in cellular network—of ideas in marketplaces or networks. These roaming networks are growing and gaining importance. Blogs number 30 million worldwide, promoted by the often-free blogging service providers like Blogger and Wordpress.

Technology with a mission

"Trying to engage audiences in conversation should be a primary goal for news organizations. It's what a democracy needs and what news organizations are meant to support," wrote the authors of Hypergene, a blog committed to furthering the concept of citizen journalism.

Lawrence Lessig, a law professor at Stanford and an Internet visionary, argues that as people become immune to traditional streamlined and broadcasted messages, blogging presents an opportunity for communities to arise, assuming that individuals must congregate around issues important to them if they are to act with power.

Lessig states ". . . the blog may be the first innovation from the Internet to make a real difference in election politics." Blogs engage people to act, he concluded.

The marketplace for technological ideas is not dissimilar from the marketplace for political ones. Lessig's reasoning applies, maybe even more so, to the technology arena where blogging is more common than in any other space, except maybe in politics.

But for Josh Quittner, who runs *Business 2.0* magazine, blogs and bloggers are positive elements in media that keep journalism honest.

"I don't think blogs are something that big media should get into. It doesn't make business sense, attracting a few thousand readers, compared to the print version, we print 630,000 copies a month and blogs should be independent voices. It is a question of credibility," he said. Yet Quittner promotes blogging among staff members. "It makes them better reporters. It widens their network and creates the basis for good analysis," he said.

The Significance of Blogs to Journalists

Blogs are goldmines for journalists doing professional and crafted work. The blogosphere is a huge source to tap, using

Ground Zero

[A] funny thing happened on the way to the Web's irrelevance: the blogging phenomenon, a grassroots movement that may sow the seeds for new forms of journalism, public discourse, interactivity and online community.

While no one is really sure where this is all heading, my hunch is that blogging represents Ground Zero of the personal Webcasting revolution. Weblogging will drive a powerful new form of amateur journalism as millions of Net users—young people especially—take on the role of columnist, reporter, analyst and publisher while fashioning their own personal broadcasting networks. It won't happen overnight, and we're now seeing only version 1.0, but just wait a few years when broadband and multimedia arrive in a big way.

J.P. Lasica, *"Blogging as a Form of Journalism,"*
Online Journalism Review, *May 24, 2001. www.ojr.org.*

services like Tecnorati.com (a blog search engine) and Googlenews, for new ideas, arguments and leads to new stories and for follow-ups on stories on other sites.

I had my first experience using blogs as a resource when I wrote a story on Pay-Pal for *CNNMoney.com* about how the company was about to enter the mobile-payment scene. Postings on jobsites revealed that Pay-Pal was hiring senior staff to lead this development within the company. After researching the company, talking to analysts and researching competition, it was clear that Pay-Pal was serious about it. The published story roamed the blogosphere and, within a week, received more than 500 posts. The sites that published the story were blogs, networks of communities with an interest in different aspects of the story—whether mobile payments, stockholders of Paypal or Ebay, who owns the company, news about the technology that evidently would be used and so on. One story became relevant to a variety of beats covering blogs.

Issues in Blogging

But there are snakes in this new media 'Garden of Eden.' Rumors seem to have a natural habitat in the blog world, as well as ranting and personal opinions. The issues of trust and reliability are difficult. In a blogpost in the *Spokesman Review*, blog reporter Ken Paulman pinpoints the issue publishers must address:

"We hold all news to the same standards, regardless of whether it's online or in print. But that raises a question: do readers hold information they read on the Internet to a different standard? Do you trust a story more because it's in black-and-white on a sheet of newsprint, or does it make a difference? What about typos and grammatical errors?"

Siliconbeat.com, a blog issued by the *San Jose Mercury News* covering the startup scene in Silicon Valley, is attracting around 10,000 readers daily. The increased readership they've experienced is based on the information being relevant, not necessarily trustworthy in a way accepted in traditional print publishing.

"We pass information to our readers that wouldn't have made the sheet" said Michael Bazeley, one of two blogging editors on Siliconbeat. "We've gained readership and interest, but we don't process the information [the same way] we do for the paper, so it's less of an effort," he said. Readers apparently feel confident that they can decipher hard news and information from opinion, but it is up to those readers.

Much of the success is also due to the blog's more free tone of voice. "Journalists who blog the way they write in the paper is not interesting" Michael Bazeley says.

"Blog responsibly, and you'll build a reputation for being a trusted news source. Don't, and you won't have a reputation to worry about," writes John Hiler.

Why Should Newspapers Blog?

Magazines and papers should consider blogging to build their legitimacy in targeted communities and societies. The transitional nature of business and media consumption must be considered if publishing houses want to prevail in their chosen markets.

By entering the blog world, papers connect to new readers via sites like Technorati. This is a way of building a new audience. *PC World*, for instance, being a big media player, is proud of being accepted in the blogosphere and referred to by other bloggers. This way, the magazine reaches readers it would not have otherwise.

Blogs can build communities, whether communities of interest or of best practice. Magazines and staff can aggregate not news, but also interests, establishing forums for dialogue among participants and strengthening the bonds to its readers.

Through blogs papers have a channel for niche content that otherwise wouldn't have found its way to readers.

Communities breed on relevant and reliable information. A newspaper or blog can grow if it provides relevant and reliable information to leaders in its targeted communities. The differences between traditional papers and blogs are that the latter can be more 'open' to their audiences, letting readers participate in making stories, and, in extreme cases, letting readers publish their own stories.

Traditional printing is an expensive process, especially in metropolitan areas. And as sites like Craigslist.org, free after text ads, demolish the traditional revenue model for papers, the cost of printing will be harder to justify. Papers are slow and money-sucking operations, or as Shel Israel, author of the book *Naked Conversations*, put it "In the Information Age, the newspaper has become a cumbersome and inefficient distribution mechanism. If you want fast delivery of news, paper is a stage coach competing with jet planes." By blogging some beats or sections that normally run in print, publications would expand their audience as well [as] attract new readers through blogging using fewer resources.

Blogs are also a way of using journalists more effectively. All information, given that it is relevant, that actually does not fit into the paper can be channeled through blogs, allowing the readers to choose what to read or not. This enables a dialogue, a sense of ownership and participation that is essential in creating communities.

Traditional big media will not become obsolete. "Blogs add a new dimension to traditional publishing," said Harry McCracken, editor-in-chief at *PC World* and the man behind *PC World's* award-winning *Techlog*. McCracken means that blogs are a low-investment and low-risk enterprise, as opposed to traditional media projects.

According to Josh Quittner, big media is still ahead. Quittner's vision is grand: "There is mass media today, and there will be class media tomorrow. The five dollars we charge today for a subscription does not even cover the distribution costs of the magazine. Ten to fifteen years ahead, when our paper is a luxury item and wanted by fewer, those that can will pay the $50 per copy price. Those that will be able to buy the magazine will be very attractive to advertisers."

A Pivotal Point

Media as a shared experience and even a co-op between producers and consumers is a novel idea and presents new opportunities, as well as new challenges. Blogs can connect new readers to a publication and keep old readers loyal. By democratizing media in this way, readers have an opportunity to "vote" instantly on issues that are relevant to them. In that regard, blogs are better off serving their democratic legacy.

For innovation journalism, blogs present a tool for analyzing trends and current events faster by having fruitful, synchronous conversations with the market. In other words, to be in the loop and, in many cases, reclaim a pivotal point in communities.

> "The vast majority of Weblogs do not provide original reporting—for me, the heart of all journalism."

Blogs Are Not Journalism

Rebecca Blood

Rebecca Blood is a writer, speaker, blogger, and the author of The Weblog Handbook: Practical Advice on Creating and Maintaining Your Blog. *In the following viewpoint, Blood rejects blogs as a form of journalism. She insists that while bloggers may provide commentary, research, eyewitness accounts, and unique perspectives, the vast majority do not provide the credible, first-hand reporting that trained journalists strive to produce. Blood instead views blogging as "participatory media," a medium that valuably takes place outside of mainstream media.*

As you read, consider the following questions:

1. According to Blood, what is fundamental to blogging?

2. What types of blogs are the most frequently cited, as stated by Blood?

3. In the author's opinion, how can blogging be an incidental form of journalism?

Rebecca Blood, "Weblogs and Journalism: Do They Connect?" *Nieman Reports*, vol. 57, no. 3, Fall 2003, pp. 61–63. Copyright © 2003 by the President and Fellows of Harvard College. Reproduced by permission.

We are entering a new age of information access and dissemination. Tools that make it easy to publish to the Internet have given millions of people the equivalent of a printing press on their desks and, increasingly, in their pockets. Unless we understand the difference between amateur reporting and personal publishing—and recognize Weblogs as just one form these activities might take—we will not be able to fully understand the implications they have for culture, journalism and society.

Let's start with the Weblog—a frequently updated Web site, with posts arranged in reverse chronological order, so new entries are always on top. Early Webloggers linked to selected news articles and Web pages, usually with a concise description or comment. The creation of software that allowed users to quickly post entries into predesigned templates led to an explosion of short-form diaries, but the reverse-chronological format has remained constant. It is this format that determines whether a Web page is a Weblog.

Note that the form preceded the software. Easy-to-use software has fueled the fast adoption of the form, but Weblogs may be created without it. The Weblog is arguably the first form native to the Web. Its basic unit is the post, not the article or the page. Bloggers write as much or as little as they choose on a topic, and although entries are presented together on the page, each post is given a permalink, so that individual entries can be referenced separately.

Hypertext is fundamental to the practice of Weblogging. When bloggers refer to material that exists online, they invariably link to it. Hypertext allows writers to summarize and contextualize complex stories with links out to numerous primary sources. Most importantly, the link provides a transparency that is impossible with paper. The link allows writers to directly reference any online resource, enabling readers to determine for themselves whether the writer has accurately represented or even understood the referenced piece. Bloggers who reference but do not link material that might, in its entirety, undermine their conclusions, are intellectually dishonest.

Are Weblogs a Form of Journalism?

The early claim, "Weblogs are a new form of journalism," has been gradually revised to "some Weblogs are doing journalism, at least part of the time." As even the enthusiasts now concede, Weblogs used to record memories, plan weddings, or coordinate workgroups can't be classified as journalism by any definition. So in any discussion about Weblogs and journalism, the first question to ask is: Which Weblogs?

The four Weblog types most frequently cited are:

• Those written by journalists;

• Those written by professionals about their industry;

• Those written by individuals at the scene of a major event;

• Those that link primarily to news about current events.

Weblogs maintained for respected news organizations will certainly qualify as journalism if they uphold the same standards as the entire organization. But some argue that independent sites maintained by journalists automatically constitute journalism, simply because their authors are journalists. A Weblog written by a journalist does not necessarily qualify as journalism for the same reason a novel written by a journalist does not: It is the practice that defines the practitioner, not the other way around. The case of Jayson Blair, fired [in 2003] from *The New York Times* for fabricating stories, illustrates that whatever the journalist's reputation or affiliation, journalism is characterized by strict adherence to accepted principles and standards, not by title or professional standing.

Some advocates of Weblogs as journalism point to the Weblogs produced by industry insiders as the future of trade journalism. They argue that, while reporters tend to rely on only a few sources even when reporting very complex stories, Weblogs written by the people working in a field will naturally convey a more complete version of the news about their profession. But those with a stake in the public perception of an issue—as working professionals invariably have—are those we can rely upon least for an unbiased perspective. Their commentary, done with integrity, can be a great source of accurate information and nuanced, informed analysis, but it will never replace the journalist's mandate to assemble a fair, accurate and complete story that can be understood by a general audience.

Personal accounts are more problematic: Is an eyewitness account journalism and, if so, when? Depending on the event? Depending on the inability of another individual to compile a more complete version of the story? Depending on the skill or training of the person writing the account? The standards used to determine when a personal recollection becomes a journalistic report are likely to vary from case to case.

This leaves link-driven sites about current events. There are certainly similarities between the practices behind these Weblogs and some of the activities required to produce a newspaper or news broadcast. Just as a newspaper editor chooses which wire stories to run, the Weblog editor chooses which stories to link. But bloggers are never in a position to determine which events will be reported. And just as opinion columnists use news accounts as a springboard to present their interpretation of events, bloggers are usually very happy to tell you what they think of what they link.

But is blogging a new form of journalism?

Frankly, no. I'm not practicing journalism when I link to a news article reported by someone else and state what I think— I've been doing something similar around the water cooler for years. I'm engaged in research, not journalism, when I search the Web for supplementary information in order to make a point. Reporters might do identical research while writing, but research alone does not qualify an activity as journalism. Bloggers may point to reader comments as sources of information about the items they post, but these are equivalent to letters to the editor, not reporting. Publishing unsubstantiated (and sometimes anonymous) e-mails from readers is not journalism, even when it's done by someone with journalistic credentials. Credible journalists make a point of speaking directly to witnesses and experts, an activity so rare among bloggers as to be, for all practical purposes, nonexistent.

Instead of inflating the term "journalism" to include everyone who writes anything about current events, I prefer the term "participatory media" for the blogger's practice of actively highlighting and framing the news that is reported by journalists, a practice potentially as important as—but different from—journalism.

Weblogs as Participatory Media

So when I say Weblogs and journalism are fundamentally different, one thing I mean is that the vast majority of Weblogs do not provide original reporting—for me, the heart of all journalism. But Joan Connell, the former executive producer for opinion and communities at MSNBC, has said she believes Weblogs are journalism only when they are edited. This will be poorly received by those journalists who have embraced the form for its freedom from professional standards and processes. Of course, bloggers unaffiliated with news organizations may state their opinions quite frankly, unworried about placating editors, offending advertisers, or poisoning relationships with sources.

When bloggers do report the news, the form is usually incidental to the practice. When policy analyst David Steven decided to document the 2002 World Summit on Sustainable Development, he set up a Weblog so that he could easily post reports on each day's events. He attended news conferences.

The Limitations of Blogging

But as the experiment progresses, the limitations of blogging have also become apparent. Bloggers tend to form online cliques and pat one another on the back. Few of them have been able to keep up the same level of quality for long periods of time: If a thousand flowers bloom in the blogosphere, many wilt fairly quickly. And though bloggers don't claim to be objective, their personal obsessions can still become grating. For example, there's a large swath of the conservative blogosphere that seems almost entirely devoted to attacking *The New York Times* and especially columnist Paul Krugman, as if no other major newspaper or columnist deserved reproach.

Chris Mooney,
"Forum: How Blogging Changed Journalism—Almost,"
Pittsburgh Post-Gazette, *February 2, 2003.*

He interviewed conference speakers. He summarized the proceedings in the Daily Summit. But this was not a triumph of the Weblog form. It was made possible by the free availability of easy-to-use publishing software. That the end product was a Weblog was irrelevant to Steven's purposes—and to those of his readers. For two weeks, Steven was on the frontline, reporting, editing and publishing news from the Summit. Journalism? I believe so, though Connell might disagree.

Perhaps the biggest reason millions of amateur writers produce Weblogs is that the easiest-to-use Web publishing tools produce only that format. Blogs have become the default choice for personal Web publishing to such a degree that the two ideas are conjoined. When commentators talk about Weblogs as the future of journalism, they sometimes seem to mean, "personal publishing is the future of journalism," or "amateur reporting is the future of journalism"—but neither of these need manifest in the Weblog form.

Whether personal publishing and amateur reporting begin to appear in different forms will depend on the availability of tools that allow nonprofessionals to create and contribute to other kinds of publications. A Korean Web site called "Ohmy-News" employs more than 26,000 "citizen reporters" who submit articles on everything from birthday celebrations to political events. The publication is credited with helping to elect South Korean President Roh Moohyun, who granted his first postelection interview to the site. This is amateur reporting, but it is not blogging.

I see the wide adoption of Weblogs as just the first wave of an age of online personal publishing. As Weblog software evolves into content management software, look for a surge of other kinds of online publications, many of which will be updated periodically instead of continually. If these publications employ a Weblog, it will be as an annotated table of contents rather than as the focus of the site. Amateur reporting will become more widespread, particularly with the proliferation of mobile devices that can upload photos and text. These devices will be pervasive, but little of this content will be widely seen, partly because there will be so much to pick through. Such content will be widely distributed only when it has the import of the Rodney King video.

Weblogs will be used in mainstream journalism, without question. But the vast majority of bloggers will continue to have a very different mandate from journalists. It is unrealistic to apply the standards of journalism to bloggers who rarely have the time or resources to actually report the news. In my book, "The Weblog Handbook," I deliberately reject the journalistic standards of fairness and accuracy in favor of transparency as the touchstone for ethical blogging. As media participants, we are stronger and more valuable working outside mainstream media, rather than attempting to mirror the purposes of the institution we should seek to analyze and supplement.

> "With the rise of [Internet] journalism,
> many more people are passing on their
> observations and ideas, playing a role
> previously occupied only by members
> of the institutional press."

Internet Journalism Will Transform the Media

Scott E. Gant

In the following viewpoint, Scott E. Gant contends that citizens and nonprofessionals engaging in journalism on the Internet are transforming the practice. From presidential scandals to the Iraq War, they have become a force in breaking news and analysis, as well as in supplying information that traditional journalists cannot, Gant states. He further suggests that more Americans are going online for their news and information, and that purposeful, serious blogs are gaining importance. Therefore, the author argues that journalism's transformation requires an extensible inclusion of Internet journalists. Gant is a Washington, DC-based attorney and author of We're All Journalists Now: The Transformation of the Press and Reshaping of the Law in the Internet Age, *from which the viewpoint is excerpted.*

As you read, consider the following questions:

1. What examples does the author provide of Internet journalists challenging mainstream media?

2. How does Gant support his claim that more Americans now consider the Internet and blogs as their source of news and information?

3. As stated by Gant, what are arguments against Internet journalism?

Although most established news organizations hate to admit it, nontraditional journalists have become a force in breaking news and analyzing it. [Internet news editor] Matt Drudge, one of the earliest and most controversial to disseminate political news and commentary through the Internet, broke the story [in 1998] about President Clinton's affair with Monica Lewinsky. His Drudge Report scooped *Newsweek*, which elected not to publish the article it was developing on the Clinton-Lewinsky relationship, and other mainstream journalism powerhouses did not even have the story to publish until after Drudge went with it. The significance of that moment in the history of American journalism is not lost on many professional journalists. Michael Kinsley, who has run the editorial page of the *Los Angeles Times* and edited the *New Republic* magazine as well as the online periodical *Slate*, commented about the Lewinsky scandal: "The Internet made this story. And this story made the Internet. Clintongate, or whatever we are going to call it, is to the Internet what the Kennedy assassination was to TV news: its coming of age as a media force."

Shaping the Media Landscape

Since then, nontraditional journalists have continued shaping the media landscape. For example, in 2002, then-Senate Majority Leader Trent Lott came under fire for praising fellow

Senator Strom Thurmond's segregationist campaign for the presidency in 1948, suggesting the nation would have been better off had Thurmond been elected. After an initial wave of criticism, the controversy abated in the mainstream media. However, bloggers continued to hammer on the story, scrutinizing Lott's legislative record on civil rights and past statements about Thurmond's 1948 candidacy, prompting traditional media outlets to pick it up again, ultimately leading to his resignation as majority leader. In 2004, contributors to the conservative blog Power Line were primarily responsible for discrediting documents used in CBS News's unflattering story about [former] President George W. Bush's National Guard service (based in part on expertise about old typewriters), ultimately casting a cloud over Dan Rather and leading to the departure of several others at CBS who worked on the piece. More recently, bloggers uncovered and publicized examples of doctored photographs published by some news organizations during the 2006 conflict between Israel and Hezbollah.

The contributions of citizens working outside established news organizations have not been limited to the disclosure of discrete facts and one-time events. For instance, bloggers—including some active-duty military personnel—have provided important coverage of the conflicts in Iraq and Afghanistan, often supplying information that could not be obtained by mainstream journalists.

There is clearly an interest in the work of these nonprofessionals. More than fifty million Americans turn daily to the Internet for news—a number that is certain to grow. Of those, many look beyond traditional news organizations as sources of information and opinion. One 2006 survey shows that 39 percent of Internet users (57 million American adults) read blogs. According to another, from early 2007, more than 80 percent of respondents view Web sites as an important source of news and information, and most believe blogging and other sources outside of established media are important to the future of journalism.

The "New" Journalists?

Are these bloggers and other nonprofessionals journalists? Not surprisingly, professional journalists and the general public tend to see things differently. According to a study conducted by the University of Pennsylvania in 2005, 81 percent of professional journalists resisted the idea that bloggers are journalists. In contrast, an informal poll of readers taken by the *Christian Science Monitor* in the same year found that 57 percent of respondents believed bloggers are journalists and deserve the protections extended to the press.

I believe the readers have the better view—at least in the sense that *some* blogging clearly constitutes journalism. Although the concept of "news" arguably transcends time and culture, journalism as an idea, and as a practice, does not. It is only for the past two or three centuries that people have regularly written and published true stories about current events. Journalism is a tool for informing one another about the world's affairs, and helping make sense of it all. Journalists are not a priestly class. They are citizens, just like the rest of us. In the United States, we are all free to write down our thoughts and share them with others. Many bloggers and others using the Internet to distribute ideas and information are engaging in the same activity as professional journalists (whether they do it as accurately, or as well, is another matter), and it hardly seems relevant that they use the Web as their method of publication, or that they may not get paid for their efforts.

The century that preceded the emergence of the Web—a period dominated by large news organizations, increasingly controlled by profit-oriented corporations—appears to have hardened an artificial distinction between professional journalists and everyone else. After an extended detour during which the means of mass communication effectively rested in the hands of the few, technological developments, with the Web at its foundation, are unwinding that process and democratizing communications as a whole, and journalism in particular.

In a sense, we are returning to where we started. The institutional press no longer possesses the exclusive means of reaching the public. Anyone can disseminate information to the rest of the world (at least anyone with computer access) at virtually no expense.

So what should we call this new breed of journalism? The list of terms used to describe it is already long and growing: Stand-alone Journalism; Grassroots Journalism; Ad Hoc Journalism; Personal Journalism; Bottom-up Journalism; Participatory Journalism; Networked Journalism; Collaborative Journalism; Open Source Journalism; "We" Journalism; "We-dia" (contrasted with Media); and Citizen Journalism (the term I generally prefer . . .).

All of these terms generally refer to forms of nontraditional journalism, typically practiced by someone who has not (at least heretofore) engaged in journalism to make a living, and who is not associated with what previously might have been viewed as a mainstream media organization. A subset—for instance, Networked or Collaborative Journalism—is, by definition, collective in nature, designed to promote and allow interactive writing and editing. This collective work is largely modeled upon, and inspired by, the success of similar efforts in creating a type of computer software called "open source" that, as the name suggests, allows free access to source code, and permits people to modify and add to the code. This process contributed to the development of the software called Linux, which successfully competes with proprietary software developed by Microsoft and other companies.

Right now traditional media organizations and citizen journalists are circling each other warily, trying to figure out the best way to deal with one another. Although professional journalists tend to have greater resources, citizen journalists have certain advantages of their own. For instance, many bloggers specialize in topics to the extent few professionals employed by media companies can, and the Web arguably

Hybrid Journalism

[Journalism professor Jay] Rosen's hybrid notion shifts the focus from defining "who is a journalist" to "what is journalism." That's a necessary shift, and once it's made, it may be possible to build a new journalism, combining, for example, the best of traditional shoe-leather reporting with exciting new citizen-journalist teams. But a hybrid would require true collaboration between old and new practitioners who are serious about sustaining journalism and its public-service mission. Old media will have to let go of some attitudes and assumptions that are no longer relevant, and new media will need to recognize standards that can infuse credibility and trust into this new journalism. Working together will require everyone in the bigger tent to drop their animosities and check their egos. It's not about us, after all. It's about keeping watch on those in power, about ensuring an informed citizenry, about maintaining a democratic culture that is strengthened by vibrant reporting on vital institutions.

Ann Cooper, "The Bigger Tent,"
Columbia Journalism Review, *September-October 2008.*

provides better error-correction mechanisms than traditional media with large numbers of "fact-checkers" weighing in at warp speed.

Amateur Hour

While recognizing some of the strengths of bloggers and their Internet brethren, many professional journalists are reluctant to view them as able to make meaningful contributions to journalism. Nicholas Lemann, dean of Columbia University's Graduate School of Journalism, drew considerable criticism from bloggers for his 2006 article in the *New Yorker*, provocatively entitled "Amateur Hour," which examined the role of nonprofessional journalists, and concluded that, as of now, "there is not much relation between claims for the possibilities inherent in journalist-free journalism and what people engaged in that pursuit are actually producing." Another Columbia professor, Samuel Freedman, was more blunt, recoiling at the notion of calling nonprofessionals "journalists," and claiming that the citizen journalism movement "forms part of a larger attempt to degrade, even to disenfranchise, journalism as practiced by trained professionals."

Similar skepticism about the virtues of journalism performed by nonprofessionals has been expressed by Fred Brown, a past president of the century-old Society of Professional Journalists, the largest of the nation's journalism associations, who wrote a "traditional journalist's" responsibility is to find and report "new and accurate information," while blogs are "good at finding flaws in others' information" and the priority of a nontraditional journalist is "to be interesting." *USA Today* columnist Andrew Kantor similarly chided "amateur" journalists for their penchant to "make up the rules as they go" and "blow small things out of proportion."

Some media observers critique bloggers and other nonprofessionals on the grounds they have a parasitic relationship with mainstream news organizations. As Richard Posner, the prolific author and federal judge, wrote in the *New York Times Book Review*, "the legitimate gripe of the conventional media is not that bloggers undermine the overall accuracy of news reporting, but that they are free riders who may in the long run undermine the ability of the conventional media to finance the very reporting on which bloggers depend."

Others decry nonprofessional journalists because they muddy the waters at a time when we need professional journalists more than ever, to filter and interpret the wealth of information available in the Internet age. Today, they claim, the press's sorting, selecting, and judging functions are more important than ever. . . .

The reluctance of mainstream media organizations to recognize nontraditional and citizen journalists as "journalists" is evident in other areas—and will play a significant role in the effort by a new and growing generation of nonprofessionals to avoid being relegated to second-class status.

The media establishment's claim of priority over other citizens is pervasive—and accepted at many levels of federal and state government. Whatever the merits of this perspective in the past, the transformation of journalism necessitates that we reconsider the practice of reflexively extending professional journalists rights and privileges not available to others engaged in the practice of journalism.

Amplifying Conversation

There is no doubt that we are all well served by having a cadre of energetic, smart, and well-funded professional journalists on the lookout for the rest of us—and there would be cause for alarm if they disappeared. But the reality is that professional journalists do not go most places, or see most things. Much of what is worth knowing, and worth thinking about, is neglected by the mainstream media. Now, with the rise of citizen journalism, many more people are passing on their observations and ideas, playing a role previously occupied only by members of the institutional press. Journalism has been elegantly described as carrying on and amplifying conversation among the people themselves. The Web and other technological advances have enabled many more of us to participate in these conversations.

Who is a journalist? Should journalists be given rights and privileges not enjoyed by other citizens? It is time for us to confront these questions directly and thoughtfully. We all have a stake in how they are answered.

*"The highest level of journalistic achieve-
ment . . . has come from old-fashioned
big-city newspapers and television networks, not Internet journalists."*

Internet Journalism Will Not Transform the Media

Nicholas Lemann

*To its advocates, Internet journalism is a profound development
because it transfers the hold on public information and discussion from traditional media to the people, writes Nicholas Lemann in the following viewpoint. However, Lemann disagrees
with the claim that Internet journalism will transform the profession. While he acknowledges that citizens have taken to the
Web and raised credible suspicions about big media and provided urgent, on-the-scene reporting, Lemann argues that most
of them do not produce original information or offer vital, daring points of view. Thus, he concludes that Internet journalism
does not take up the challenge to power that professional journalism does. Lemann is the dean and Henry R. Luce Professor at
the Journalism School at Columbia University.*

Nicholas Lemann, "Amateur Hour," *The New Yorker*, August 7, 2006. Copyright © 2006
by the author. All rights reserved. Reproduced by permission of the author.

As you read, consider the following questions:

1. According to Lemann, how do bloggers define themselves?

2. What historical phenomenon does the author compare to Internet journalism?

3. What examples does Lemann provide of popular and acclaimed Internet journalism?

On the Internet, everybody is a millenarian [having a belief in a coming ideal society]. Internet journalism, according to those who produce manifestos on its behalf, represents a world-historical development—not so much because of the expressive power of the new medium as because of its accessibility to producers and consumers. That permits it to break the long-standing choke hold on public information and discussion that the traditional media—usually known, when this argument is made, as "gatekeepers" or "the priesthood"—have supposedly been able to maintain up to now. "Millions of Americans who were once in awe of the punditocracy now realize that anyone can do this stuff—and that many unknowns can do it better than the lords of the profession," Glenn Reynolds, a University of Tennessee law professor who operates one of the leading blogs, Instapundit, writes, typically, in his new book, *An Army of Davids: How Markets and Technology Empower Ordinary People to Beat Big Media, Big Government and Other Goliaths.*

The rhetoric about Internet journalism produced by Reynolds and many others is plausible only because it conflates several distinct categories of material that are widely available online and didn't use to be. One is pure opinion, especially political opinion, which the Internet has made infinitely easy to purvey. Another is information originally published in other media—everything from Chilean newspaper stones and entries in German encyclopedias to papers presented at Micronesian conferences on accounting methods—which one can find instantly on search and aggregation sites. Lately, grand journalistic claims have been made on behalf of material produced specifically for Web sites by people who don't have jobs with news organizations. According to a study published last month [July 2006] by the Pew Internet & American Life Project, there are twelve million bloggers in the United States, and thirty-four percent of them consider blogging to be a form of journalism. That would add up to more than four million newly minted journalists just among the ranks of American bloggers. If you add everyone abroad, and everyone who practices other forms of Web journalism, the profession must have increased in size a thousandfold over the last decade.

Citizen Journalism

As the Pew study makes clear, most bloggers see themselves as engaging only in personal expression; they don't inspire the biggest claims currently being made for Internet journalism. The category that inspires the most soaring rhetoric about supplanting traditional news organizations is "citizen journalism," meaning sites that publish contributions of people who don't have jobs with news organizations but are performing a similar function.

Citizen journalists are supposedly inspired amateurs who find out what's going on in the places where they live and work, and who bring us a fuller, richer picture of the world than we get from familiar news organizations, while sparing us the pomposity and preening that journalists often display. Hong Eun-taek, the editor-in-chief of perhaps the biggest citizen-journalism site, Oh My News, which is based in Seoul and has a staff of editors managing about forty thousand volunteer contributors, has posted a brief manifesto, which says, "Traditional means of news gathering and dissemination are quickly falling behind the new paradigm. . . . We believe news is something that is made not only by a George W. Bush or a Bill Gates but, more importantly, by people who are all allowed to think together. The news is a form of collective thinking. It is the ideas and minds of the people that are changing the world, when they are heard."

That's the catechism, but what has citizen journalism actually brought us? It's a difficult question, in part because many of the truest believers are very good at making life unpleasant for doubters, through relentless sneering. Thus far, no "traditional journalist" has been silly enough to own up to and defend the idea of belonging to an élite from which ordinary citizens are barred. But sometimes one will unwittingly toss a chunk of red meat to the new-media visionaries by appearing not to accord the Internet revolution the full measure of respect it deserves—as John Markoff, a technology reporter for the *Times*, did in 2003 in an interview with *Online Journalism Review*. Jeff Jarvis, a veteran editor, publisher, and columnist, and, starting in September [2006], a professor at the City University of New York's new journalism school, posted the interview on his blog, BuzzMachine, with his own post-facto reactions added, so that it reads, in part, this way:

MARKOFF: I certainly can see that scenario, where all these new technologies may only be good enough to destroy all the old standards but not create something better to replace them with. I think that's certainly one scenario.

JARVIS: Pardon me for interrupting, but that made no frigging sense whatsoever. Can you parse that for me, Mr. Markoff? Or do you need an editor to speak sense? How do new standards "destroy" old standards? Something won't become a "standard" unless it is accepted by someone in power—the publishers or the audiences. This isn't a game of PacMan.

MARKOFF: The other possibility right now—it sometimes seems we have a world full of bloggers and that blogging is the future of journalism, or at least that's what the bloggers argue, and to my mind, it's not clear yet whether blogging is anything more than CB radio.

JARVIS: The reference is as old-farty and out-of-date as the sentiment. It's clear that Markoff isn't reading weblogs and doesn't know what's there.

Hey, fool, that's your *audience* talking there. You should want to listen to what they have to say. You are, after all, spending your living writing for *them*. If you were a reporter worth a damn, you'd care to know what the marketplace cares about. But, no, you're the mighty NYT [*New York Times*] guy. You don't need no stinking audience. You don't need ears. You only need a mouth.

To live up to its billing, Internet journalism has to meet high standards both conceptually and practically: the medium has to be revolutionary, and the journalism has to be good. The quality of Internet journalism is bound to improve over time, especially if more of the virtues of traditional journalism migrate to the Internet. But, although the medium has great capabilities, especially the way it opens out and speeds up the discourse, it is not quite as different from what has gone before as its advocates are saying. . . .

In fact, what the prophets of Internet journalism believe themselves to be fighting against—journalism in the hands of an enthroned few, who speak in a voice of phony, unearned authority to the passive masses—is, as a historical phenomenon, mainly a straw man. Even after the Second World War, some American cities still had several furiously battling papers, on the model of "The Front Page." There were always small political magazines of all persuasions, and books written in the spirit of the old pamphlets, and, later in the twentieth century, alternative weeklies and dissenting journalists like I. F. Stone. When journalism was at its most blandly authoritative—probably in the period when the three television broad-

Journalism Will Never Go Out of Style

Even in a bleak period for journalism, you can find signs of vitality—the astounding growth of NPR [National Public Radio]; the development of Salon and Slate on the Internet; the transformation of *USA Today* from an object of ridicule to a serious, successful national paper; the opening of twenty-four-hour cable news operations in local as well as metropolitan markets.

So don't think journalism is going away. Delivery systems may change from paper to computer, and reporters may be renamed "content providers." Revered and beloved publications may perish while reality-TV series thrive. But intellectual curiosity, vigorous research, acute analysis, and elegant prose will never go out of style. If anything, the shorter the supply, the more those traits will be valued.

Samuel J. Freedman, Letters to a Young Journalist. *New York: Basic Books, 2006.*

cast networks were in their heyday and local newspaper monopoly was beginning to become the rule—so were American politics and culture, and you have to be very media-centric to believe that the press established the tone of national life rather than vice versa.

A Mere Safety Valve?

Every new medium generates its own set of personalities and forms. Internet journalism is a huge tent that encompasses sites from traditional news organizations; Web-only magazines like *Slate* and *Salon*; sites like Daily Kos and NewsMax, which use some notional connection to the news to function as influential political actors; and aggregation sites (for instance, Arts & Letters Daily and Indy Media) that bring together an astonishingly wide range of disparate material in a particular category. The more ambitious blogs, taken together, function as a form of fast-moving, densely cross-referential pamphleteering—an open forum for every conceivable opinion that can't make its way into the big media, or, in the case of the millions of purely personal blogs, simply an individual's take on life. The Internet is also a venue for press criticism ("We can fact-check your ass!" is one of the familiar rallying cries of the blogosphere) and a major research library of bloopers, outtakes, pranks, jokes, and embarrassing performances by big shots. But none of that yet rises to the level of a journalistic culture rich enough to compete in a serious way with the old media—to function as a replacement rather than an addendum.

The most fervent believers in the transforming potential of Internet journalism are operating not only on faith in its achievements, even if they lie mainly in the future, but on a certainty that the old media, in selecting what to publish and broadcast, make horrible and, even worse, ignobly motivated mistakes. They are politically biased, or they are ignoring or suppressing important stories, or they are out of touch with ordinary people's concerns, or they are merely passive transmitters of official utterances. The more that traditional journalism appears to be an old-fashioned captive press, the more providential the Internet looks. . . .

Still: Is the Internet a mere safety valve, a *salon des refusés*, or does it actually produce original information beyond the realm of opinion and comment? It ought to raise suspicion that we so often hear the same menu of examples in support of its achievements: bloggers took down the 2004 "60 Minutes" report on President Bush's National Guard service and, with it, Dan Rather's career; bloggers put Trent Lott's remarks in apparent praise of the Jim Crow era front and center, and thereby deposed him as Senate majority leader.

The best original Internet journalism happens more often by accident, when smart and curious people with access to means of communication are at the scene of a sudden disaster. Any time that big news happens unexpectedly, or in remote and dangerous places, there is more raw information available right away on the Internet than through established news organizations. The most memorable photographs of the London terrorist bombing last summer [2005] were taken by subway riders using cell phones, not by news photographers, who didn't have time to get there. There were more ordinary people than paid reporters posting information when the tsunami first hit South Asia, in 2004, when Hurricane Katrina hit the Gulf Coast, in 2005, and when Israeli bombs hit Beirut this summer [2006]. I am in an especially good position to appreciate the benefits of citizen journalism at such moments, because it helped save my father and stepmother's lives when they were stranded in New Orleans after Hurricane Katrina: the citizen portions of the Web sites of local news organizations were, for a crucial day or two, one of the best places to get information about how to drive out of the city. But, over time, the best information about why the hurricane destroyed so much of the city came from reporters, not citizens.

Eyewitness accounts and information-sharing during sudden disasters are welcome, even if they don't provide a complete report of what is going on in a particular situation. And that is what citizen journalism is supposed to do: keep up with public affairs, especially locally, year in and year out, even when there's no disaster. Citizen journalists bear a heavy theoretical load. They ought to be fanning out like a great army, covering not just what professional journalists cover, as well or better, but also much that they ignore. Great citizen journalism is like the imagined Northwest Passage—it has to exist in order to prove that citizens can learn about public life without the mediation of professionals. But when one reads it, after having been exposed to the buildup, it is nearly impossible not to think, *This* is what all the fuss is about?

Proudly Minor

Oh My News seems to attract far more readers than any other citizen-journalism site—about six hundred thousand daily by its own count. One day in June [2000], readers of the English-language edition found this lead story: "Printable Robots: Advances in Inkjet Technology Forecast Robotic Origami," by Gregory Daigle. It begins:

> From the diminutive ASIMO from Honda to the colossus in the animated film *Iron Giant*, kids around the world know that robots are cool yet complex machines. Advances in robotics, fuel plans from NASA that read like science fiction movie scripts.
>
> Back on Earth, what can we expect over the next few years in robot technology for the consumer?
>
> Reprogram your Roomba? Boring.
>
> Hack your Aibo robot dog? Been there.
>
> Print your own robot? Whoa!

On the same day, Barista of Bloomfield Avenue, the nom de Web of Debbie Galant, who lives in a suburban town in New Jersey and is one of the most esteemed "hyperlocal bloggers" in the country, led with a picture from her recent vacation in the Berkshires. The next item was "Hazing Goes Loony Tunes," and here it is in its entirety:

> Word on the sidewalk is that Glen Ridge officialdom pretty much defeated the class of 2007 in the annual senior-on-freshman hazing ritual yesterday by making the rising seniors stay after school for several minutes in order to give

freshmen a head start to run home. We have reports that seniors in cars, once released from school, searched for slow-moving freshman prey, while Glen Ridge police officers in cars closely tracked any cars decorated with class of 2007 regalia. Of course, if any freshman got pummelled with mayonnaise, we want to know about it.

What is generally considered to be the most complete local citizen-journalism site in the United States, the Northwest Voice, in Bakersfield, California (which also has a print version and is owned by the big daily paper in town), led with a story called "A Boost for Business Women," which began:

So long, Corporate World.

Hello, business ownership—family time, and happiness.

At least, that's how Northwest resident Jennifer Meadors feels after the former commercial banking professional started her own business for Arbonne International, a skin care company, about eight months ago. So far, it's been successful, professionally and personally. . . .

In other words, the content of most citizen journalism will be familiar to anybody who has ever read a church or community newsletter—it's heartwarming and it probably adds to the store of good things in the world, but it does not mount the collective challenge to power which the traditional media are supposedly too timid to take up. Often the most journalistically impressive material on one of the "hyperlocal" citizen-journalism sites has links to professional journalism, as in the Northwest Voice, or Chi-Town Daily News, where much of the material is written by students at Northwestern University's Medill School of Journalism, who are in training to take up full-time jobs in news organizations. At the highest level of journalistic achievement, the reporting that revealed the civil-liberties encroachments of the war on terror, which has upset the Bush Administration, has come from old-fashioned big-city newspapers and television networks, not Internet journalists; day by day, most independent accounts of world events have come from the same traditional sources. Even at its best and most ambitious, citizen journalism reads like a decent Op-Ed page, and not one that offers daring, brilliant, forbidden opinions that would otherwise be unavailable. Most citizen journalism reaches very small and specialized audiences and is proudly minor in its concerns. David Weinberger, another advocate of new-media journalism, has summarized the situation with a witty play on Andy Warhol's maxim: "On the Web, everyone will be famous to fifteen people."

Reporting Requires Reporters

Reporting—meaning the tradition by which a member of a distinct occupational category gets to cross the usual bounds of geography and class, to go where important things are happening, to ask powerful people blunt and impertinent questions, and to report back, reliably and in plain language, to a general audience—is a distinctive, fairly recent invention. It probably started in the United States, in the mid-nineteenth century, long after the Founders wrote the First Amendment. It has spread—and it continues to spread—around the world. It is a powerful social tool, because it provides citizens with an independent source of information about the state and other holders of power. It sounds obvious, but reporting requires reporters. They don't have to be priests or gatekeepers or even paid professionals; they just have to go out and do the work.

The Internet is not unfriendly to reporting; potentially, it is the best reporting medium ever invented. A few places, like the site on Yahoo! operated by Kevin Sites, consistently offer good journalism that has a distinctly Internet, rather than repurposed, feeling. To keep pushing in that direction, though, requires that we hold up original reporting as a virtue and use the Internet to find new ways of presenting fresh material—

which, inescapably, will wind up being produced by people who do that full time, not "citizens" with day jobs.

Journalism is not in a period of maximal self-confidence right now, and the Internet's cheerleaders are practically laboratory specimens of maximal self-confidence. They have got the rhetorical upper hand; traditional journalists answering their challenges often sound either clueless or cowed and apologetic. As of now, though, there is not much relation between claims for the possibilities inherent in journalist-free journalism and what the people engaged in that pursuit are actually producing. As journalism moves to the Internet, the main project ought to be moving reporters there, not stripping them away.

Periodical Bibliography

The following articles have been selected to supplement the diverse views presented in this chapter.

Mark Brandel   "Information Overload: Is It Time to Go on a Data Diet?" *Computerworld*, August 25, 2008.

Edward B. Driscoll Jr.   "Medium Cool: A Blog Is Simply a Web Log, or Diary, That One Shares With Others. But When Users Were Finally Able to Add Video to These Blogs, a Viral Phenomenon Was Born," *Videomaker*, February 2009.

Terry Golway   "Print's Demise," *America*, November 3, 2008.

John Hazlehurst   "Daily Newspapers Are in Decline Across Country," *Colorado Springs Business Journal*, February 13, 2009.

Catherine Holahan   "Heard It Through the Newsvine," *Business Week Online*, October 10, 2007.

Miha Kovac   "Never Mind the Web. Here Comes the Book," *LOGOS: The Journal of the Book Community*, July 2008.

Josh Levine   "Turning the Page," *Time International*, March 2, 2009.

Erik Oatman   "Blogomania!" *School Library Journal*, August 2005.

Natasha Spring and William Briggs   "The Impact of Blogging: Real or Imagined?" *Communication World*, May–June 2006.

Joe Strupp   "Caught in the Web," *Editor & Publisher*, August 1, 2007.

Dan Tynen   "Eight Ways Twitter Will Change Your Life," *PC World*, November 2008.

For Further Discussion

Chapter 1

1. Media Matters for America alleges that conservatives dominate newspaper columns in the United States. In your opinion, is the importance of a newspaper advantage increasing or decreasing? Explain your answer.

2. Ian Jobling argues that mainstream news exaggerates racism and prejudice against minorities. In your view, does Elizabeth Llorente overstate biases against ethnic media professionals and groups? Use examples from the viewpoints to support your answer.

3. Brian Fitzpatrick insists that the scarcity of news media outlets is a myth. Does Steve Rendall successfully counter this claim, in your opinion? Why or why not?

Chapter 2

1. Charlie Cray maintains that mass media is under increasing corporate control and consolidation. By contrast, Ben Compaine proposes that media outlets are more diverse and accessible than ever. In your view, who makes the most compelling claim? Use examples from the viewpoints to develop your answer.

2. Common Cause argues that cross-ownership leads to the degradation of news and media content. In your opinion, does James L. Gattuso effectively argue against this assertion? Explain your answer.

Chapter 3

1. Hillary Rodham Clinton, unlike Katherine Sternheimer, believes that studies have proven that media violence is linked to youth violence. In your opinion, which author

presents the most convincing position? Provide examples from the viewpoints to support your answer.

2. David J. Hanson refutes the findings of the Center on Alcohol Marketing and Youth (CAMY) that establish links between alcohol advertising and underage drinking. In your view, are RAND Corporation's findings more, less, or equally as credible as CAMY's? Use examples from the viewpoints to develop your answer.

Chapter 4

1. Are the characteristics of a surviving newspaper that Philip Meyer and Bill Keller describe similar or dissimilar? Use examples from the viewpoints to develop your answer.

2. Do you concur with Rebecca Blood's statement that part of the value of blogging is that it takes place outside of journalism? Why or why not?

3. To support his argument that citizen journalism does not stand up to journalistic standards and achievements, Nicholas Lemann provides clips written by people who are not trained journalists. In your view, do these examples fairly reflect the quality and integrity of so-called citizen journalism as a whole? Explain your answer.

Organizations to Contact

The editors have compiled the following list of organizations concerned with the issues debated in this book. The descriptions are derived from materials provided by the organizations. All have publications or information available for interested readers. The list was compiled on the date of publication of the present volume; the information provided here may change. Be aware that many organizations take several weeks or longer to respond to inquiries, so allow as much time as possible.

American Advertising Federation (AAF)
1101 Vermont Ave. NW, Suite 500
Washington, DC   20005-6306
(202) 999-2231 • fax: (202) 898-0159
e-mail: aaf@aaf.org
Web site: www.aaf.org

AAF is a professional advertising association representing corporate advertisers, agencies, media companies, suppliers, and academia. The organization protects and promotes the well-being of advertising. In addition, AAF's college-chapter program has 226 affiliated chapters in the United States and abroad.

American Civil Liberties Union (ACLU)
125 Broad St., 18th Fl., New York, NY   10004
Web site: www.aclu.org

The ACLU champions the rights set forth in the Declaration of Independence and the Constitution, and it opposes censoring any form of speech. The ACLU publishes several handbooks, public policy reports, project reports, civil liberties books, and pamphlets. It also offers the online resource, "StandUp!" a Web page for students.

American Library Association (ALA)
50 E. Huron, Chicago, IL   60611
(800) 545-2433
e-mail: ala@ala.org
Web site: www.ala.org

ALA is the oldest and largest library association in the world. It works to protect intellectual freedom and to promote high-quality library and information services. ALA publishes the *Newsletter on Intellectual Freedom*, pamphlets, articles, posters, and an annually updated Banned Books Week Resource Kit.

Center for Investigative Reporting (CIR)
2927 Newbury St., Suite A, Berkeley, CA   94703
(510) 809-3160
Web site: http://centerforinvestigativereporting.org

CIR is a nonprofit news organization composed of journalists dedicated to encouraging investigative reporting. It conducts investigations, offers consulting services to news and special-interest organizations, and conducts workshops and seminars for investigative journalists. Its publications include the *Muckraker Blog* and numerous reporting guides.

Electronic Frontier Foundation (EFF)
454 Shotwell St., San Francisco, CA   94110-1914
(415) 436 9333 • fax: (415) 436 9993
e-mail: eff@eff.org
Web site: www.eff.org

EFF is an organization of students and other individuals that aims to promote a better understanding of telecommunications issues. It fosters awareness of civil liberties issues arising from advancements in computer-based communications media, and the organization supports litigation to preserve, protect, and extend First Amendment rights in computing and telecommunications technologies. EFF's publications include the electronic newsletter *EFFector Online*, and online bulletins and publications.

Fairness and Accuracy in Reporting (FAIR)
112 W. 27th St., New York, NY 10001
(212) 633-6700 • fax: (212) 727-7668
e-mail: fair@fair.org
Web site: www.fair.org

FAIR is a national media watchdog group that offers documented criticism of media bias and censorship. The organization believes that the mass media is controlled by, and thereby supports, corporate and governmental interests and that media organizations are insensitive to women, labor, minorities, and other special-interest groups. FAIR publishes the bimonthly magazine *Extra!*

Federal Communications Commission (FCC)
445 12th St. SW, Washington, DC 20554
(888) 225-5322
Web site: www.fcc.gov

Established by the Communications Act of 1934, the FCC is an independent U.S. government agency charged with regulating interstate and international communications by radio, television, wire, satellite and cable. The FCC's jurisdiction covers the 50 states, the District of Columbia, and U.S. possessions. The FCC publishes the *Daily Digest*, which provides a brief synopsis of Commission orders, news releases, speeches, public notices and all other FCC documents that are released each business day.

Freedom Forum
555 Pennsylvania Ave. NW, Washington, DC 20001
(202) 292-6100
e-mail: news@freedomforum.org
Web site: www.freedomforum.org

The Freedom Forum is a research organization dedicated to studying the media and educating the public about their influence on society. It publishes an annual report and as well as numerous publications on free speech, freedom of information, newsroom diversity, and media ethics.

Media Institute

2300 Clarendon Blvd., Suite 503, Arlington, VA   22201
(703) 243-5700 • fax: (703) 243-8808
e-mail: info@mediainstitute.org
Web site: www.mediainstitute.org

The Media Institute is a nonprofit research foundation that specializes in communications policy issues. The organization fosters three goals: freedom of speech, deregulation of the media and communications industry, and excellence in journalism. Its publications include *Media Consolidation, Regulation, and the Road Ahead,* and *Television Violence and Aggression: Setting the Record Straight.*

Media Research Center (MRC)

25 S. Patrick St., Alexandria, VA   22314
Web site: www.mrc.org

The Media Research Center is a conservative media watchdog organization concerned with what it perceives to be a liberal bias in the news and entertainment media. In 1995, it opened the Parents Television Council to bring family programming back to television. MRC publishes the newsletters *Media Reality Check* and *Notable Quotables.*

National Association of Black Journalists (NABJ)

University of Maryland, 8701-A Adelphi Rd.
Adelphi, MD   20783-1716
(866) 479-6225 • fax: (301) 445-7101
e-mail: nabj@nabj.org
Web site: www.nabj.org

Founded in 1975, the National Association of Black Journalists serves to strengthen ties among African American journalists, promote diversity in newsrooms, and honor the achievements of black journalists. It publishes the *NABJ Journal.*

National Institute on Media and the Family
606 24th Ave. South, Suite 606, Minneapolis, MN   55454
(888) 672-5437 • fax: (612) 672-4113
Web site: www.mediafamily.org

The Institute seeks to educate and inform the public and to encourage practices and policies that promote positive change in the production and use of mass media. It does not advocate censorship of any kind, aiming to partner with parents and other caregivers, organizations, and corporations to create good media choices for families.

Poynter Institute
801 Third St. South, St. Petersburg, FL   33701
(888) 769-6837 • fax: (727) 553-4680
Web site: www.poynter.org

The Poynter Institute is a school dedicated to teaching and inspiring journalists and media leaders. It promotes excellence and integrity in the practice of craft and in the practical leadership of successful businesses. It stands for a journalism that informs citizens and enlightens public discourse. The Institute carries forward founder Nelson Poynter's belief in the value of independent journalism.

Bibliography of Books

Bonnie M.
Anderson

News Flash: Journalism, Infotainment, and the Bottom-Line Business of Broadcast News. San Francisco: Jossey-Bass, 2004.

Ben Bagdikian

The New Media Monopoly. Boston: Beacon Press, 2004.

Michael A. Banks

Blogging Heroes: Interviews with 30 of the World's Top Bloggers. Indianapolis: Wiley Publishing, 2008.

Pablo J.
Boczkowski

Digitizing the News: Innovation in Online Newspapers. Cambridge, MA: MIT Press, 2004.

L. Brent Bozell

Weapons of Mass Distortion: The Coming Meltdown of the Liberal Media. New York: Three Rivers Press, 2005.

Asa Briggs and
Peter Burke

A Social History of the Media: From Gutenberg to the Internet. 2nd ed. Malden, MA: Polity, 2005.

Thomas de
Zengotita

Mediated: How the Media Shapes Our World and the Way We Live in It. New York: Bloomsbury Publishing, 2005.

David Edwards
and David
Cromwell

Guardians of Power: The Myth of the Liberal Media. London: Pluto Press, 2006.

Robert Erikson
and Kent Tedin
American Public Opinion: Its Origins, Content, and Impact. Updated 7th ed. New York: Pearson/Longman, 2007.

Dan Gilmore
We the Media: Grassroots Journalism by the People, for the People. Sebastopol, CA: O'Reilly, 2006.

Tom Goldstein
Journalism and Truth: Strange Bedfellows. Chicago: Northwestern University Press, 2007.

Doris A. Graber
Media Power in Politics. 5th ed. Washington, DC: CQ Press, 2007.

Neil Henry
American Carnival: Journalism under Siege in an Age of New Media. Berkeley, CA: University of California Press, 2007.

Henry Jenkins
Convergence Culture: Where Old and New Media Collide. New York: NYU Press, 2006.

Steven Johnson
Everything Bad Is Good for You: How Popular Culture Is Making Us Smarter. New York: Riverhead Trade, 2005.

Lawrence Lessig
Free Culture: How Big Media Uses Technology and the Law to Lock Down Culture and Control Creativity. New York: Penguin, 2004.

Charles M.
Madigan, ed.
30: The Collapse of the American Newspaper. Chicago: Ivan R. Dee, 2007.

| David W. Moore | *The Opinion Makers: An Insider Exposes the Truth Behind the Polls.* New York: Beacon Press, 2008. |

| Patrick R. Parsons | *Blue Skies: A History of Cable Television.* Philadelphia: Temple University Press, 2008. |

| Neil Postman | *Amusing Ourselves to Death: Public Discourse in the Age of Show Business.* 20th anniversary ed. New York: Penguin Books, 2005. |

| Metta Spencer | *Two Aspirins and a Comedy: How Television Can Enhance Health and Society.* Boulder, CO: Paradigm Publishers, 2006. |

Index

N